6/1/2001.   50l.

D0476438

The Nature of Hell

A Report by the Evangelical Alliance's Commission on Unity and Truth among Evangelicals (ACUTE)

The Nature of Hell

acute

Copyright © 2000 Evangelical Alliance
Whitefield House, 186 Kennington Park Road, London SE11 4BT

This edition printed in 2000 by Acute
Acute is an imprint of Paternoster Publishing,
P.O. Box 300, Carlisle, Cumbria, CA3 OQS, U.K.
and Paternoster Publishing USA P.O. Box 1047, Waynesboro,
GA 30830-2047
http: www.paternoster-publishing.com

British Library Cataloguing in Publication Data
A catalogue record for this book is available from the British Library.

ISBN 0-95329-922-8

Cover Design by Mainstream, Lancaster
Typeset by WestKey Ltd, Falmouth, Cornwall
Printed in Great Britain by Cox & Wyman
Cardiff Road, Reading, Berkshire, RG1 8EX

Contents

About ACUTE

ACUTE is committed to an ongoing programme of research and publication on theological issues which are of concern to evangelicals.

The next report to appear from ACUTE will look at the subject of faith and prosperity.

For details and information on this and other forthcoming reports, contact ACUTE (Publications) Evangelical Alliance, 186 Kennington Park Road, London SE11 4BT.

e-mail acute@eauk.org

Telephone 020 7207 2100

Fax 020 7207 2150

Note on Referencing

The first mention of a source in the footnotes gives full details of that source. Subsequent mentions of more frequently-cited sources are abbreviated. For abbreviated titles see Bibliography.

Preface

The following report is the result of a two-year study on hell by a working group of ACUTE – the Alliance Commission on Unity and Truth among Evangelicals. ACUTE was established by the Evangelical Alliance in 1995 to work for consensus on theological issues that test evangelical unity, and to provide, on behalf of evangelicals, a co-ordinated theological response to matters of wider public debate. As well as Evangelical Alliance members, ACUTE's Steering Group includes representatives of the British Evangelical Council and the Evangelical Movement of Wales.

As we explain in the Introduction, the nature of hell has become a significant focus of theological disagreement among evangelicals throughout the last decade or so. In some cases, the disagreement has caused division and hurt. With this in mind, during 1994–5 the Alliance convened informal discussions of the matter between various evangelical theologians and church leaders, some of whom produced preliminary papers. With the formation of ACUTE, it was decided to continue this process and, after further background dialogue, an introductory feature on hell was published in the summer 1997 edition of the Alliance's magazine *Idea*, setting out the main lines of divergence. This early work was co-ordinated by the first convenor of ACUTE, the Rev Dave Cave, and the authors of this report would like to thank him for laying the ground for what follows.

When the Rev Dr David Hilborn took over as Convenor of ACUTE in July 1997, it was decided that a more formal process of research, consultation and reporting on hell would be needed. To this end, in January 1998 our working group was assembled. We met on seven occasions up to April 1999, and produced a draft report which was circulated for peer review. The names of the peer reviewers are listed below. The report was then presented to, and discussed by, EA's Council of Management on 16th September 1999. After a full morning session, the Council commended it to Alliance members and others for 'study, reflection and constructive response'.

Thanks are due to the Rev Robert Amess and Mr Pradip Sudra, who originally formed part of the working group but had to step down due to other commitments. We should also like to commend Miss Carolyn Skinner for the ever-efficient administrative support she provided. The Rev Dr Derek Tidball, Mr Roger Forster and Dr Peter Kimber spoke diversely and illuminatingly to the report at the Council meeting, for which we are very grateful. In addition, the following people kindly acted as peer reviewers: Mr Nik Ansell (Institute for Christian Studies, Toronto); Mr Ray Bromham (University of Wales); Dr Chris Cook (University of Kent); Dr John Colwell (Spurgeon's College, London); Dr Martin Davie (Oak Hill College, London); Mr Martyn Eden (Public Affairs Director, Evangelical Alliance); Miss Caroline Fletcher (University of Sheffield); Mr Roger Forster (Ichthus Christian Fellowship); Mr Arfon Jones (Former General Secretary, EA Wales); Prof Donald Mcleod (Free Church of Scotland Theological College, Edinburgh); Dr Stephen Mosedale (Methodist Church); Prof Paul Helm (King's College, London); Dr Stephen Travis (St. John's College, Nottingham); Dr Nigel Wright (Altrincham Baptist Church, formerly Spurgeon's College, London). Their comments proved most helpful in the refining of the text, but it should not be assumed that they agree with all its findings.

Finally, we would like to express our gratitude to Mark Finnie and his colleagues at Paternoster Press for their help, kindness and forbearance through what has been a challenging process of theological reflection on a topic which most of us would rather avoid, but which Scripture compels us to face.

The Working Group

Rev Dr David Hilborn (Theological Adviser, Evangelical Alliance. Working Group Convenor and Report Editor)

Mrs Faith Forster (Ichthus Christian Fellowship, Evangelical Alliance Executive Committee and representative on World Evangelical Fellowship)

Dr Tony Gray (Universities and Colleges Christian Fellowship)

Dr Philip Johnston (Tutor in Old Testament, Wycliffe Hall, Oxford)

Mr Tony Lane (Director of Research and Senior Lecturer in Historical Theology, London Bible College)

Foreword

Most people shy away from the subject of hell. It has always been a difficult topic, but the increasing pluralism of Western culture has made it more of a stumbling block than ever. It would be no exaggeration to say that both within and outside the church many now see the doctrine of hell as indefensible and obsolete. Growing numbers of Christian theologians are advocating universalism; the 'new age' movement has popularised eastern understandings of reincarnation, and there are still plenty of humanists rejecting any notion of life after death.

All this presents evangelicals with a serious challenge. Our identity is formed in large part by our commitment to the uniqueness of Jesus Christ and to the supreme authority of the Bible. While artists and preachers may have sometimes sensationalised it, there can be little doubt that the concept of hell is a biblical one. Indeed, the uncomfortable truth is that Jesus himself taught more about hell than anyone else in Scripture. This means that we cannot simply ignore it, or deny its reality. Yet at the same time, there has been considerable debate among evangelical scholars about the proper interpretation of scriptural teaching on this issue. This debate goes back at least 150 years, but in the last decade or so it has intensified around the precise nature of hell itself – specifically whether hell is a realm of everlasting conscious punishment for each individual who goes there, or whether the suffering of the unredeemed in hell will eventually result in their extinction.

During my time as UK Director, and now General Director, the hell debate has become a growing concern for the Evangelical Alliance. I am therefore delighted that ACUTE has produced the following report. It is a clear, well-researched guide to the arguments, which admirably demonstrates the Alliance's commitment to biblical truth and unity. It aims to inform those who have not thought through the issue yet, but also offers those with strong convictions an opportunity to test their stance once more against the biblical witness, rather than against tradition or culture alone.

Along with our Council of Management, I commend this report to Alliance members and others for study, reflection and constructive response.

Rev Joel Edwards
General Director, Evangelical Alliance UK

Introduction: Evangelicals and the Debate About Hell

What happens when we die? This is one of the great questions of life. It has prompted diverse responses from philosophers, artists, scientists and religious leaders. In the Christian context, however, it has most typically been answered in terms of a decisive contrast – the contrast between heaven and hell. The gospels teach that heaven is the realm of God from which Jesus himself came to earth, and to which he returned after his death and resurrection (John 3:13; Luke 24:51). Jesus' own teaching also stresses that heaven is the eternal reward of all who believe and follow him (Matt. 5:12; 19:21; Luke 10:20). We shall come to see below that the ultimate destiny of the saved is more precisely cast as a holy city, New Jerusalem, which descends from a renewed heaven to a renewed earth (Rev. 21–2). Yet however exactly we depict the fate of the redeemed, it is a fate which stands in stark contrast to that faced by those whom the Bible calls 'impenitent', 'unrighteous' or 'wicked'. The 'hell' which awaits such people is the domain of the devil and his hordes – a sphere of damnation, punishment, anguish, and destruction (Matt. 5:12; 10:28; 18:9; 23:33; 25:31–46; Luke 12:5; 16:23; Jas. 3:6; 2 Pet. 2:4). This basic distinction is clear, and the Church from its inception has characteristically commended Christ's gospel as the 'hope of heaven', while warning that those who reject it are on the 'road to hell' (cf. Matt. 7:13; 16:18–19).

All this has serious consequences. The promise of eternal life and heavenly bliss may constitute good news for the Church and the world; but for most people – Christians included – the matter of hell is both difficult and uncomfortable. However much it is used as a casual expletive, and however much people reserve it for the worst of criminals, hell is deeply disturbing. As one writer has observed, 'any who have a right to discuss [it] wish they did not have to'; and as another has remarked, 'there is no more unpalatable subject in Christian theology'.[1] Nonetheless, these are not valid reasons to ignore it. The fact that Scripture witnesses to the reality of hell, and the fact that Jesus himself teaches more on it than anyone else in the Bible, mean that Christians are obliged to deal with it. This is true not least of *evangelical* Christians, for whom the witness of Scripture and the example of Jesus are central in terms of authority.[2]

But there are more specific reasons why the Evangelical Alliance Commission on Unity and Truth has undertaken to produce this report now.

Traditionally, evangelical Christians have understood the Bible to teach that hell is a place of unending physical and psychological punishment, and that with the possible exceptions of children who die in infancy, the mentally disabled and those who never hear the gospel, it awaits all who die without faith in Jesus Christ.[3] As we demonstrate in Chapter 4,

1. Fudge, W., *The Fire That Consumes: The Biblical Case for Conditional Immortality (Revised Edn.)*, Carlisle: Paternoster, 1994 [1982], p. 1; Dowsett, Dick, *God, That's Not Fair!* Carlisle: OM Publishing, [1982] 1998, Preface.

2. For key definitions of evangelical priorities in relation to Scripture and Christology see Bebbington, D.W., *Evangelicalism in Modern Britain: A History from the 1730s to the 1980s,* London: Unwin Hyman, 1989, pp. 2–19; McGrath, Alister E., *Evangelicalism and the Future of Christianity,* London: Hodder & Stoughton, 1994; Knight, H.K. III, *A Future for Truth: Evangelical Theology in a Postmodern World,* Nashville: Abingdon Press, 1997, pp. 17–35.

3. We shall deal with these 'classic exceptions' in Section 5 below. For accounts of the evangelical tradition on this subject see Peterson, R.A., *Hell on Trial: The Case*

evangelicals have thereby followed a tradition articulated by early church fathers like Tertullian, Jerome and Augustine, by medieval theologians such as Anselm and Thomas Aquinas, and by the mainline Protestant Reformers.[4] Latterly, however, this view has been challenged by alternative explanations which, though traceable to previous periods of church history, have begun to influence evangelicalism to an unprecedented degree.

Until quite recently, the greatest challenge to the traditional doctrine of eternal conscious punishment came from **universalism**. Rather than holding to the unending torment of the wicked, the third century theologian Origen proposed that everything, perhaps even Satan and his angels, would eventually be restored to God. This doctrine of *apokatastasis*, with its hope in the 'restitution of all things', did not exclude the possibility of hellfire and divine condemnation, but saw them as remedial rather than penal.[5]

As we shall demonstrate in Chapter 2, universalism has taken several forms. In the modern age, however, it has become a distinguishing mark of theological liberalism. Indeed, it is significant for our purposes that when the Evangelical Alliance was formed in 1846, a clause was added to the original draft of its doctrinal basis in order to align the new body with eternal punishment and against a then-emergent liberal universalism.[6]

---

3. (*continued*) *for Eternal Punishment*, Phillipsburg: P&R Publishing, 1995, pp. 97–117; Rowell, Geoffrey, *Hell and The Victorians*, Oxford: Clarendon, 1974, and Powys, David, 'The Nineteenth and Twentieth Century Debates about Hell and Universalism', in N.M. de S. Cameron (ed.), *Universalism and the Doctrine of Hell*, pp. 93–138; idem, *'Hell': A Hard Look at a Hard Question*, Carlisle: Paternoster, 1997.

4. For more detail on this tradition see Bauckham, R., 'Universalism: A Historical Survey', *Themelios* 4:2 (January 1979), p. 48; Peterson, R.A., *Hell on Trial*, pp. 97–138.

5. Origen, *De Principiis (On First Principles)*, Trans. G.W. Butterworth. London: SPCK, 1936, 6:1–2.

6. For an account of this, see Kessler, J.B.A. Jnr., *A Study of the Evangelical Alliance in Great Britain*. Goes: Oosterbaan & Le Cointre, 1968, pp. 67–69. The additional clause affirmed 'The Immortality of the Soul, the Resurrection of the Body, the

It is also pertinent that this clause became central to a dispute in 1868 which led the Honorary Secretary of the British EA, T.R. Birks, to resign, having published a book which was construed as leaning too far in a restitutionist direction.[7]

As it is, universalism has never gained acceptance among any more than a tiny minority of evangelicals. There are signs that this minority may be growing somewhat, and in Chapter 2 we shall assess this growth in the context of contemporary pluralism and syncretism. Nonetheless, while the universalist view may suit the spirit of our age, we shall confirm that it is inconsistent with evangelical faith. In particular, we shall show that it diverges seriously from the doctrinal bases of those key evangelical bodies which comprise ACUTE: the Evangelical Alliance, the British Evangelical Council and the Evangelical Movement of Wales.

A far more immediate challenge to traditional evangelical understanding is posed by what has come to be known as **conditional immortality** or **conditionalism**. This has a more recent lineage than universalism, and is apparently closer to the historic mainstream position.[8] Conditionalists argue that the concept of the 'eternal soul' which underpins the traditional view owes more to Platonist thought than to biblical teaching. Rather than accepting that unbelievers will suffer endless conscious punishment in hell at the hands of a wrathful God, conditionalists read Scripture as teaching that the unrighteous will ultimately be destroyed, or annihilated. For some, this annihilation is related to the point of death. Most evangelical conditionalists, however, hold that it will take place after a period of punishment in a hell which will itself pass away once

---

6. (*continued*) Judgment of the World by our Lord Jesus Christ, with the Eternal Blessedness of the Righteous, and the Eternal Punishment of the Wicked'. For comparisons between this and other inter-evangelical statements on hell, see Appendix.

7. Kessler, *Evangelical Alliance*, pp. 67–69.

8. For histories of conditionalism see Blanchard, John, *Whatever Happened to Hell?* Darlington: Evangelical Press, pp. 211–14; Rowell, *Hell and The Victorians*; Powys, 'Hell and Universalism', pp. 93–138.

God has recreated the universe. Not only do they see this as more consistent with the actual vocabulary of the relevant texts, and with God's grand plan of salvation; they also argue that it more adequately reflects his character as a God of love, mercy and justice. For these reasons, conditional immortality is sometimes identified as **annihilationism** – although annihilation of the wicked is better understood as *one consequence* of conditional immortality rather than a full definition of it. Indeed, we shall see in Chapter 5 that belief in the final annihilation of the unrighteous need not always depend on conditionalist assumptions. These caveats notwithstanding, 'conditionalism' is now commonly used in the evangelical debate to cover both 'mortalist' views of the soul and belief in the eventual extinction of the unredeemed. Except when technical distinctions need to be made between these two points, we shall therefore also use 'conditionalism' in this general way.

Conditionalism has attracted much greater attention within evangelical circles since 1988. In that year, the prominent evangelical statesman and writer John Stott revealed for the first time in print that he was drawn towards the idea that the impenitent will be destroyed rather than condemned to eternal conscious punishment.[9] Stott stated that he held this view 'tentatively' and that he would not 'dogmatise' about it.[10] He also appeared somewhat uncertain about the specific conditionalist route to annihilation.[11] Even so, his comments

---

9. Stott, John & Edwards, David L., *Essentials: A Liberal-Evangelical Dialogue*, London: Hodder & Stoughton, 1988, pp. 287–304; 312–329.

10. Stott, *Essentials*, p. 320.

11. Stott agrees with the conditionalist premise that immortality of the soul is 'a Greek not a biblical concept', and that immortality is granted by God rather than being natural to humanity (p. 316). He diverges, however, from the view that sinners are extinguished at the point of death, which he appears to associate with 'conditionalism', and favours instead the view that 'everybody survives death and will even be resurrected, but the impenitent will finally be destroyed', which he distinguishes as 'annihilationist' rather than 'conditionalist' (p. 316, 320). We shall see in Chapter 5, however, that this is a somewhat misleading division, since most

sparked a world-wide debate – one which continues to exercise evangelical theologians.[12] The impact of this debate may
be reflected in a recent theological survey of 848 Evangelical
Alliance member churches, which showed conditionalism to
be a minority view, but a not insignificant one.[13]

With hindsight, it appears that an emergent 'evangelical
conditionalism' may have been one factor in the revision of the
Evangelical Alliance's Basis of Faith during the period
1967–70. This revision replaced the 1846 clause on eternal
punishment with two more general affirmations. The first of
these states that fallen humanity is 'subject to God's wrath and
condemnation'. The second declares that sin has 'eternal
consequences'.[14] As they stand, these amendments appear to
permit conditionalist as well as traditionalist interpretation,
since annihilation can be said to be eternal in *consequence*, if not

---

11. (*continued*) conditionalists accept that 'death' in Scripture is not confined to
the termination of earthly life, but can refer to *ultimate* extinction at the 'second
death' – that is, following final judgment and a time of divine punishment in hell.

12. For accounts of this debate and its origins in the Stott-Edwards dialogue, see
Gray, Tony, 'Destroyed For Ever: An Examination of the Debates Concerning
Annihilation and Conditional Immortality', *Themelios* 21:2 (January 1996),
pp. 14–18; Peterson, *Hell on Trial*, pp. 11–14.

13. In the survey, conducted in summer and autumn 1998, 79.6% of responses
(675 churches) affirmed the statement, 'Those who die without faith in Jesus face
eternal punishment in hell', while 14.2% (121 churches) affirmed the statement,
'Those who die without faith in Jesus will be annihilated'. Surveys were intended
to reflect the view of the congregation as a whole. It is likely, however, that many
were in fact completed by the minister or leadership team, and that levels of consultation with individual church members would have varied. The final figures can
therefore only be taken as a guide to the convictions of EA's membership on hell.

14. The full texts of the two clauses are as follows: 'The universal sinfulness and
guilt of fallen man, making him subject to God's wrath and condemnation', and
'The substitutionary sacrifice of the incarnate Son of God as the sole and all-suffi-
cient ground of redemption from the guilt and power of sin, and from its eternal
consequences'. These effectively replaced the 1846 clause on hell, which endorsed
'The immortality of the soul, the Resurrection of the Body, the Judgment of the
world by our Lord Jesus Christ, with the Eternal Blessedness of the Righteous, and
the Eternal Punishment of the wicked'. For comparisons with other inter-
evangelical statements on hell, see Appendix.

duration. Having said this, the current form of the EA Basis makes it difficult to draw definitive conclusions in this area, because it has no clause devoted to general resurrection, final judgment and heaven and hell *as such*. We believe that the inclusion of such a clause might be helpful, not least as a means to clarifying what we take to be an implicit openness to conditionalism in the present wording of the Basis. At the same time, it should be stressed that the British Evangelical Council and the Evangelical Movement of Wales maintain statements of faith which unequivocally affirm eternal punishment.[15] This underlines that the following report is not the product of a working group and theological commission who were agreed on all aspects of hell before the text was written. Nor, indeed, do we agree on all aspects of the issue now. On the contrary, we recognise that the subject of hell is one on which evangelicals have genuine and deeply felt differences. Even so, as well as articulating those differences, we have sought here to define our common convictions on the matter, and to indicate a positive and realistic way forward.

In dealing with the subject before us, we begin by identifying issues which lie in the background of the specific debate about hell as such – namely death, final resurrection, judgment, the intermediate state, purgatory and the scope of salvation. We then turn to the witness of Scripture, and introduce those texts that are most pertinent for a clear understanding of the nature of hell itself. Next we trace how these texts have been interpreted through church history. We move on from this to a detailed account of the contemporary debate on hell, defining the main positions adopted by evangelical thinkers and assessing how these positions are established exegetically and theologically. In the closing chapters we consider the pastoral

---

15. Clause 6 of the BEC Doctrinal Basis affirms: 'The everlasting punishment of the lost'. Clause vii of the EMW statement of Doctrinal Belief states: 'The unbelieving will be condemned by [God] to hell, where eternally they will be punished for their sins under the righteous judgment of God.' For other inter-evangelical statements on hell, see Appendix.

dimensions of the debate and examine the implications of current disagreement on hell for evangelical unity. We end with conclusions and recommendations designed to address this problem.

In presenting this study, we are aware that ACUTE does not have the authority of a denominational doctrine commission or an ecclesiastical court. Neither it, nor its sponsoring body the Evangelical Alliance, can compel belief in the things affirmed and asserted here. Nor can it formally anathematise or excommunicate those who disagree with its conclusions. Rather, the document which follows attempts to provide information on the debate about hell, and to offer considered guidance to evangelicals on how hell can be defined within the parameters of biblical and doctrinal orthodoxy. In particular, we seek to identify limits to the interpretation of the EA Basis of Faith on this matter. We are also keen that hell should be treated not only as a concern of dogmatic theology, but also as a significant factor in the mission and ministry of the Church. To this end, we offer practical advice as well as formal definition.

As evangelicals committed to the supreme authority of the Bible, we believe that hell is a profound biblical concern which must not be neglected. As those who believe that theology matters, we make no apology for broaching this difficult issue at a time when it is either widely ignored, or redefined in ways that bear little relation to biblical teaching or classical church tradition. Even so, we recognise that our report is by no means the last word on this matter, and would invite prayerful, biblically grounded responses to it as part of the ongoing debate.

2

Background Issues in the Hell Debate

Before focussing specifically on hell, we need to be clear that Scripture presents it as a consequence of certain *other* events and processes. There is broader agreement among evangelicals about these events and processes than about the nature of hell itself – but a summary of them will help to place the hell debate in context. As we proceed with this summary, it will be useful to comment in passing on issues, such as reincarnation and purgatory, which have no part in evangelical doctrine, but which evangelicals often encounter in missionary and apologetic contexts. We shall also at this point consider universalism, which offers a response to the problem of hell, but which does so either by denying its existence altogether, or by finally neutralising its force.

Death as a Prelude to Hell

First, Scripture is clear that entry into heaven or hell is something that follows death. In Christopher Marlowe's early seventeenth century tragedy *Dr Faustus*, Mephistopheles declares of life on earth, 'Why, this is hell, nor am I out of it.'[1] Likewise, the modern existentialist Jean-Paul Sartre famously

---

1. *Dr Faustus* (1604), Act I, Scene 3.

had a character in his play *No Exit* define hell as 'other people'.[2] Indeed, 'hell' has regularly been used as a metaphor for this-worldly strife. As far as Scripture is concerned, however, hell is fundamentally a post-mortem phenomenon.

Jesus himself recognised that human beings must undergo physical death, and although he offered 'salvation' from its eternal effects, he viewed the actual process of dying as inevitable for believers and unbelievers alike (Matt. 10:28; Luke 6:9, 12:4). Indeed, his own willingness to die on the cross as a representative of and substitute for humanity confirmed that death is a universal fact of life (Mark 10:45; John 12:32–3). While theologians may diverge on whether the human *soul* is inherently eternal, there is little doubt that our earthly *bodies* must perish. Granted, in the Old Testament Enoch and Elijah appear to be exceptions to this rule (Gen. 5:24; 2 Kings 2:11). Granted, too, at least some of those left alive at Jesus' return will 'not taste death' (Matt. 16:28). But the witness of both Old and New Testaments is that death results directly from the disobedience of Adam and Eve – that is, from the rebellion of humanity against God in Eden and from the sin which thenceforth pervades life on earth (Gen. 2:17; 3:19; Rom. 5:12,17; 6:23). Death is therefore the direct consequence of living in a fallen world – something which Christians and non-Christians alike must face. So when heaven or hell are depicted in Scripture, it is either stated or assumed that their occupants have already died (Luke 16:19–31, 23:43; 2 Cor. 5:8; Phil. 1:23; Rev. 6:9).

Hebrews 9:27 has featured prominently in classical evangelical accounts of the last things. Its assertion that human beings are 'destined to die once, and after that to face judgment' has been taken to confirm that there is no way back for those who die as unredeemed sinners, and that from this point such sinners are bound inexorably for hell. As we shall see later, a few self-professed evangelicals have more recently argued that the same text need not preclude a post-mortem 'second chance'

---

2. *Huis Clos* (1944), Scene 5: '. . . l'Enfer, c'est les Autres'.

for at least some non-Christians.[3] Even they, however, would accept that the principle of 'one earthly life – one earthly death' must preclude the possibility of *reincarnation*. Nevertheless, growing sympathy for this idea in contemporary Western culture makes a brief assessment of it worthwhile.

Hell versus Reincarnation

Although reincarnation is most commonly associated with ancient eastern religions, and most particularly with Hinduism and Buddhism, it has been adopted more recently in Western Theosophist and 'new age' belief-systems. In Hindu culture it is referred to as *Samsara* and is derived from the principle that people must reap what they sow. As expounded in the *Brihadaranyakya Upanishad*, it asserts that individuals create their next life after the pattern of those desires, hopes, aspirations, failures, disappointments, achievements and actions which characterise their present life.

Integral to this belief in a series of lives is the transmigration of souls, or *metempsychosis. Metempsychosis* entails the possibility that the souls of humans inhabit the bodies of animals, and this explains why some adherents of it are vegetarians. One appeal of reincarnation is that it offers successive chances for redemption after death. Another is that it seeks to answer the charges of injustice that are often brought against God by those who have suffered badly in this life. If it seems that evil has gone unpunished and good unrewarded, then the next life, the next reincarnation, may allow the moral account to be settled. Plato, for example, commended the immortality of the soul on the basis that a soul which ceases to exist at death cannot pay the punishment due

3. E.g. Wright, Nigel, *The Radical Evangelical*, London: SPCK, 1996, pp. 98–99. See also Pinnock, Clark H., 'The Finality of Jesus Christ in a World of Religions', in Mark A. Noll and David F. Wells (eds.), *Christian Faith and Practice in the Modern World*, Grand Rapids: Eerdmans, 1988, pp. 165–67.

for its wickedness.[4] This concern for justice beyond the grave has remained central in Western defences of reincarnation.[5]

By contrast, a Christian critique of reincarnation could allege that its cycle of death and re-birth is in fact more fear-some than even a doctrine in which dead sinners are consigned irrevocably to hell. Granted, both Buddhist and Hindu thought envisage a final transcendence of this cycle, but such *Moksa* or *Nirvana* may yet take an inordinately long time to achieve. Indeed, some may never achieve it. Besides, it rests on a fundamentally works-driven model of salvation which is at odds with the Christian gospel message of salvation by grace through faith.

Despite these points of divergence, forms of reincarnation have found some advocates within the Church. Origen's restitutionism proposed that human souls pre-existed their earthly form, had fallen from a heavenly realm into an earthly existence as part of their punishment, and would ultimately be released into eternal bliss. Although he accepted that this process would take some time, he saw it unfolding through a succession of lives experienced in different universes. Lacking biblical support for this doctrine, Origen looked to Neoplato-nist philosophy, and its conviction that the soul is the essential element of human anthropology. From this point of view, such a succession of lives seemed plausible. Although it is unclear whether Origen believed on these grounds that there would be more than one *incarnation* for human beings, this is at least a plausible inference to be drawn from his theology.[6] Certainly,

---

4. An early attack by a Christian on this and other related Platonic ideas comes from Aeneas of Gaza, in his dialogue *Theophrastus*. The ideas of reincarnation, the eternity of creation, and the pre-existence of souls before their bodily life, are all criticised here. For further details see Daley, Brian E., *The Hope of the Early Church: A Handbook of Patristic Eschatology*, Cambridge: Cambridge University Press, pp. 190–92.
5. For an account of later interest in Platonic ideas on the transmigration of souls in England see Walker, D.P., *The Decline of Hell: Seventeenth-Century Discussions of Eternal Torment*, London: Routledge & Kegan Paul, 1964, pp. 104–77.
6. Daley, *Hope*, p. 58.

other early church theologians, such as Evagrius of Pontus, followed Origen's tentative signals, and hinted at the potential of souls to achieve successive incarnations.[7]

While Origen clearly moved beyond Scripture, others have more recently sought to find warrant for reincarnation in the biblical text. For example, in Matthew 17.10–13 Jesus identifies John the Baptist as 'Elijah'. On this basis, the popular mid-twentieth century preacher Leslie Weatherhead suggested that 'it would be difficult to explain such a passage other than by supposing that they regarded John the Baptist as a reincarnation of Elijah'.[8] Yet this ignores the well-established belief to which we have already alluded, that Elijah had been taken directly into heaven before his death (2 Kings 2:11). It also overlooks the fact that in Hebrew thought he was identified symbolically, rather than reincarnationally, with the expected Messiah (Mal. 4:5). Additionally, some have taken the disciples' assumption that the blind man in John 9:1–3 was blind due to his own sin as a sign that reincarnation featured in Jewish understanding at the time.[9] Whatever the substance of this claim, however, it is clear that Jesus himself repudiates this assumption and presents sin as a general problem to be solved in the present, rather than the legacy of a 'previous life'.

In our own period, the pluralist theologian John Hick has mooted the idea that reincarnation might more fairly redefine the biblical concept of 'eternal life'.[10] In addition, the Oxford philosopher of religion Richard Swinburne has tentatively accepted that it might apply to those whose characters remain

---

7. Daley, *Hope*, p. 91.

8. Weatherhead, Leslie D., *The Christian Agnostic*, London: Hodder & Stoughton, 1965, p. 209; See also *Life Begins at Death*, Nutfield: Denham House Press, 1969, pp. 70–79.

9. For a discussion of this point see Hick, John, *Death and Eternal Life*, London: Collins, 1976, pp. 367–8. See also Westcott, Brooke Fosse, *The Gospel According to St. John*, Grand Rapids: Baker Book House, 1908 [1980], p. 31–32, and Beasley-Murray, George R., *John*, Waco: Word, 1987, pp. 154–55, both of whom consider a possible link to the apocryphal text Wisdom of Solomon 8:19–20.

10. Hick, *Death and Eternal Life*, pp. 365–73.

inadequately developed in this life.[11] Other contemporary theologians in the Christian tradition have expressed openness to metempsychosis, even if their approach has been qualified at certain points.[12]

The problem with these attempts to Christianise the concept of reincarnation is that they depart from the basic biblical teaching with which we began – the teaching which holds that, in redemptive terms, death constitutes a decisive and irreversible step towards final judgment. As we have stressed, the orthodox Christian understanding has consistently been that earthly human life only occurs once for each individual. Therefore any notion of coming back in another form, at another place, or another time, is ruled out.

Central to the Buddhist notion of reincarnation in particular is the gradual denigration and loss of self. Here, progress through various different lives is taken to minimise the self and thus to be absorbed into 'the ultimate'. Christian eschatology, however, proceeds in a quite different direction – one in which believers inherit a resurrected life similar to that exhibited by Jesus, and become the true persons they were meant to be. Indeed, this resurrection life is one in which personality and personhood are made complete, rather than being diminished (Rev. 22:4).

Most crucially of all, the dominant Christian understanding of salvation is one of grace, where acceptance into eternity with God is never on the basis of one's own merits, but always through God's undeserved forgiveness of sin. In stark contrast to the progressive (or possibly regressive) cycle of reincarnation, biblical teaching denies that any succession of lives is possible beyond death. As Paternoster succinctly puts it, 'Origen, and the moderns who find Hindu and Buddhist

---

11. Swinburne, R., *The Evolution of the Soul*, Oxford: Clarendon Press, 1986, p. 302.

12. E.g. Jathanna, Origen, *The Decisiveness of the Christ-Event and the Universality of Christianity in a World of Religious Plurality*, Berne: Peter Lang, 1982; Howe, Q. Jnr., *Reincarnation for the Christian*. Philadelphia, 1994; MacGregor, Geddes, *Reincarnation as a Christian Hope*, London: Macmillan, 1982; Haring, Hermann & Metz, Johann–Baptist (eds.), *Reincarnation or Resurrection?* Concilium, 1993(5).

thought attractive, take a too optimistic view of human nature.'[13] Indeed, the orthodox Christian understanding sees human nature as fundamentally 'under judgment', and inevitably lost without the intervening mercy of God (Rom. 5:12ff.).

Death and Resurrection in Relation to Judgment

Although physical death is a decisive and necessary precursor to heaven and hell until Jesus returns, the specific fate of the deceased is sealed by divine *judgment*. In a very general sense, judgment takes place *before* death, as people are convicted of their sins (cf. Rom. 1:18–28). But there is also a more specific sense in which death itself functions as the first act in the drama of judgment, since it decisively closes off the possibility of salvation and lays bare the dire and eternal consequences of a godless life (Rom. 6:23).

The most important phase of judgment in relation to heaven and hell, however, is the judgment depicted in the New Testament as the judgment that is yet to come (Acts 17:31; Rom. 2:5–10; 2 Tim. 4:1; 1 Pet. 4:5; Rev. 20:11–15). This is that final reckoning of the 'last day', when Jesus will return in glory and exercise the judicial authority granted to him by God the Father (John 5:30). Although some have assumed that such final judgment applies only to non-Christians, the New Testament consistently depicts it as something which Christian believers must undergo as well (Matt. 13:30; 25:31–36; 2 Cor. 5:10). Indeed, it is portrayed as following a 'general resurrection' of both the unrighteous *and* the righteous. In this resurrection, the bodies of the dead will be reconstituted and raised to face the verdict of Christ, along with those who are still alive at his return (Dan. 12:12; John 5:27–29; Acts 24:15; Rom. 8:23; 1 Cor. 6:13–20; 1 Cor. 15:23ff.; Phil. 3:20–21; Rev. 20:11–15).[14]

---

13. Paternoster, M., *Thou Art There Also*, London: SPCK, 1967, p. 50.

14. Pre-millennialists infer a distinct interval (the 'millennium' of Rev. 20:1–6) between the judgment of Christians and non-Christians.

The Criteria of Final Judgment

The distinction between the redeemed and the unredeemed at
final judgment will be based fundamentally on whether or not
they have been justified by grace through faith in Christ (John
12:48; cf. Rom. 3:28). In this process, the New Testament hints
that God may take account of different peoples' relative
knowledge of the gospel (Matt. 11:21–24; Rom. 2:12–16).
Even so, it is a cardinal tenet of evangelical doctrine that
salvation is a divine rather than a human initiative. Or as the
doctrinal basis of the Evangelical Alliance puts it, the justification of the sinner occurs 'solely by the grace of God through
faith in Jesus Christ crucified and risen from the dead'.

If these points are clear, it must be admitted that evangelical
Christians often fail to acknowledge the plain teaching of
Scripture that the *final judgment itself* will be a judgment which
takes account of how people have *behaved* (Matt. 19:28f.;
25:31–46; John 5:28f.; Rom. 2:5–11; 2 Cor. 5:10; Rev. 20:12).
While this may seem confusing, the picture is clarified when
one distinguishes *justification*, which is achieved objectively for
Christians by Jesus' atoning death, from *judgment*, which deals
with all people on the basis of how they have lived their lives.
Apart from the objective justifying work of Christ, our own
good deeds are ultimately ineffective for salvation itself – but
this does not mean that they are unimportant. In fact, believers
whose lives display them are 'rewarded' at Christ's coming in
glory (Matt. 16:27). Indeed, both traditionalist and conditionalist evangelicals have argued on the basis of texts such as
Luke 10:12 and 12:47–48 that the reward received by any
believer will be proportional to his or her own works, just as
the punishment of sinners in hell will reflect the gravity of the
evil they have done on earth.[15] We shall see later that the two
groups diverge on how exactly this notion of proportionality

15. E.g. Berkhof, Louis, *Reformed Dogmatics, Vol 2*, Grand Rapids: Eerdmans, 1932,
p. 345; Shedd, W.G.T., *Doctrine of Endless Punishment*, New York: Scribner, 1886,
p. 131 n. 1; Fudge, *Fire*, pp. 117–8. Contrast Blomberg, Craig, 'Eschatology and the
Church: Some New Testament Perspectives', *Themelios* 23:3 (1998), 3–26.

should be interpreted in relation to the *length of sentence* imposed after death for sins committed in a finite life. It is also worth noting that certain other texts suggest that God's calculations on this matter may differ radically from those assumed by humans (cf. Matt. 20:1–16).

One question that arises from this classical evangelical account of the relation between justification by faith and judgment by works concerns the value of good deeds done by the unsaved. What is the purpose of such deeds if they have no part in securing eternal life? The historic evangelical response on this point holds that because God is righteous, he looks for righteousness in *all* quarters – even among those who have not put their faith in him. Hence his judgment of all people's works is a demonstration of his own absolute justice and a reminder that good deeds redound to his glory rather than to the glory of those who perform them.[16]

The Judgment of the Saved

If good works alone cannot effect the redemption of *un*believers, it must nonetheless be stressed that believers who neglect such works will be dealt with severely at the final judgment. Evangelicals have long differed on whether Christians can actually *lose* their salvation on the basis of passivity, apathy or wilful renunciation. Arminians have traditionally held this to be a possibility, and have pointed for support to texts such as Matthew 24:13; John 15:6; Hebrews 2:3f., 4:1f., 6:1–9 and Revelation 2:5. Specifically in relation to hell, they have emphasised that Jesus' teaching in this area is directed mostly towards existing disciples, and that these disciples are warned of the condemnation that awaits them if they fail to nurture and steward the gifts that God has given (cf. Matt. 25:31–46; John 5:28–9).[17] By contrast, Calvinists have maintained that God

---

16. Milne, Bruce, A., *Know the Truth*, Leicester: IVP, 1982, pp. 271–73.
17. See, for example, Pawson, David, *The Road to Hell*, London: Hodder & Stoughton, 1992, pp. 48–53; Pinnock, Clark H., 'The Finality of Christ in a World

will never relinquish those whom he has once saved. This position also has its signature texts, e.g. John 10:28; Romans 8:30, 39 and 1 Peter 1:5.[18]

It is not the purpose of this report to rehearse this debate in detail. It is clearly crucial in respect of the *criteria* by which people are supposed to enter heaven or hell, and is thus indispensable for an understanding of *soteriology* (the doctrine of salvation). However, it does not directly impinge on the nature of *hell itself,* and it is this which will be our focus here. What is clear is that *both* positions underline the reality of death for all except those still alive when Christ returns, and the deep significance of works in the last judgment.

Punishment Beyond Death Itself

If evangelicals differ on whether salvation can be lost, they are virtually unanimous in affirming that the punishment which issues from the last judgment extends beyond death, rather than merely being constituted by *death itself.* Indeed, Christian theologians in general, and evangelical theologians in particular, reject the view that the fate of the unredeemed comprises simply 'immediate extinction' – that is, annihilation at the very point of death itself without subsequent resurrection to judgment. Thus in an extensive survey of theological work on hell, David Powys concludes that annihilation at death has 'no consistent advocates'.[19] It is true that Christadelphians teach

17. (*continued*) of Religions', in Mark A. Noll & David F. Wells (eds.), *Christian Faith and Practice in the Modern World*, Grand Rapids: Eerdmans, 1988, p. 166.

18. For recent exposition of Calvinist and Arminian views on this matter see respectively Kendall, R.T., *Once Saved, Always Saved*, Belfast: Ambassador, [1983] 1992 and Pawson, David, *Once Saved, Always Saved?* London: Hodder & Stoughton, 1996.

19. Powys, 'Hell and Universalism', pp. 93–138. Even so, in peer review of this document, Stephen Mosedale moots the possibility of arguing this position from texts such as Jn. 6:40, 'which seems to lack any weight if the truth is that all will be raised up and some will be subsequently annihilated'. He adds, 'Another line of argument might be around whether "all will be judged" implies all will appear

immediate extinction for unbelievers, but as with various other Christadelphian doctrines, this falls outside mainstream Christianity.[20] As it is, evangelical conditionalists characteristically hold that the unsaved will be destroyed either soon after general resurrection and adverse final judgment,[21] or following a more protracted period of divine retribution.[22] A key text cited in defence of this position is John 5:28–9, which identifies resurrection to life and condemnation as occurring after the dead have heard Christ's voice and come out of their graves.[23]

The Intermediate State

Given their belief that death and resurrection to final judgment are distinct events separated by a clear period of time, evangelicals have generally accepted that there must be *some* sort of intermediate state between the two. Although others have found in texts such as Matthew 9: 24; John 11:11; 1 Corinthians 15:6ff. and 1 Thessalonians 4:13 a warrant for suggesting

19. (*continued*) alive before the judgment seat; after all we are familiar with posthumous pardons in our law court so is it inconceivable that unbelievers are judged *in absentia* at the judgment seat of Christ, to have the verdict of their final death ratified?'.

20. Cf. John Blanchard and R.T. Kendall, who appear not to differentiate between this marginal, cult-associated view and the views of more mainstream conditionalists, who see extinction as following either soon after general resurrection and final judgment (Constable, Aldwinckle, Stott, Hughes), or after general resurrection, final judgment and a lengthy period of punishment (Froom, Fudge, White, Atkinson, Guillebaud). Blanchard, *Whatever*, p. 213; Kendall, R.T., 'Foreword', in Buchanan, Alex, *Heaven and Hell*, Tonbridge: Sovereign World, 1995, p. 6.

21. For expositions of this view see Constable, H. *Hades; or the Intermediate State of Man*, London: Kellaway and Co., 1875 (2nd. Edn); Aldwinckle, R., *Death in the Secular City: Life after Death in Contemporary Theology and Philosophy*, Grand Rapids: W.B. Eerdmans, 1974; Stott, *Essentials*; Hughes, P.E., *The True Image: The Origin and Destiny of Man in Christ*, Leicester: IVP, 1989; Powys, David, *'Hell': A Hard Look at a Hard Question*, Carlisle: Paternoster, 1997.

22. E.g. Guillebaud, H.E., *The Righteous Judge: A Study of the Biblical Doctrine of Everlasting Punishment*, Taunton: Phoenix, 1964; Fudge, *Fire*.

23. E.g. Powys, *Hard Look*, pp. 360ff.; Fudge, *Fire*, p. 130.

that this intermediate state comprises an unconscious existence or 'soul sleep', evangelicals have mostly cited texts such
as Luke 23:43; 2 Corinthians 5:8; Philippians 1:23 and
Hebrews 12:23 in defence of the view that everyone who dies
goes immediately to either heaven or hell, and continues to
exist there consciously until they are later 'clothed' with their
resurrection bodies on the Last Day.[24] Hence in W.G.T. Shedd's
definition, 'the intermediate state for the saved is heaven without the body, and the final state for the saved is heaven with the
body ... the intermediate state for the lost is hell without the
body, and the final state for the lost is hell with the body'.[25]

While evangelical conditionalists have either approved this
sequence of events or declined to comment on it,[26] it could be
seen to challenge their particular rejection of soul-body dualism. Detailed analysis of this matter lies beyond the scope of our
report, but we would note that more work could fruitfully be
done on it by those seeking to relate the traditionalist-
conditionalist debate on hell to wider issues of eschatology.

Purgatory

The doctrine of 'purgatory' has divided Christians through the
centuries, and in particular has been one of the major divisions
between Protestants and Roman Catholics. Luther may have
remained nominally attached to it at the time of his 95 Theses
(1517),[27] but he soon came to denounce its propagation by the

---

24. For a helpful account of the issues involved here see Grudem, Wayne, *Systematic Theology*, Leicester, IVP, 1994, pp. 816–24.

25. *Endless Punishment*, p. 59.

26. The conditionalist Edward Fudge takes no exception to Shedd's sequence:
Fire, 1994. John Wenham appears to accept it also: *The Enigma of Evil*, Leicester:
IVP, 1985, p. 34. David Powys, however, is unconvinced that 1 Cor. 15 advocates an
intermediate state between death and hell: *Hard Look*, p. 253. Most other evangelical apologetics for conditionalism appear not to comment directly on the intermediate state.

27. Luther, Martin, '95 Theses' (Article 22) in Mark A. Noll (ed.), *Confessions and
Catechisms of the Reformation*, Leicester: Apollos, 1991, p. 31.

Church of Rome as inimical to the Gospel. His fellow Reformers went on to reject it decisively.[28] In reaction, it was re-affirmed at the 25th Session of the Council of Trent in 1563.[29]

Central to the concept of purgatory is the conviction that most Christians do not go straight to heaven at the point of death, but must first undergo a period of 'purification' (Latin: *purgatorium*). It should be emphasised that this process is for those who have already had their ultimate salvation assured. The doctrine of purgatory has occasionally been linked to a doctrine of 'second chance' – that is, a doctrine in which those who do not profess faith in Christ in this life may receive the opportunity to repent in the next.[30] We shall examine 'second chance' theories more closely in Chapter 6, since they have been advocated by some evangelical theologians as an alternative to the traditional view of hell. They are not, however, part of the official Roman doctrine of purgatory.

Augustine is widely credited with systematising the doctrine of purgatory and establishing its place within Roman Catholic dogma. It is expounded definitively in his *City of God* (21.13, 16, 24), and is related to prayers for the dead in his *Confessions* (9.13.34–37).[31] Both he and Caesarius of Arles found apologetic warrant for purgatory in 1 Corinthians

---

28. Luther, Martin, 'A Commentary on St. Paul's Epistle to the Galatians (1531)', in John Dillenberger (ed.), *Martin Luther: Selections from His Writings*, New York: Anchor, 1961, p. 113–14. For an account of other Reformers' views see Cameron, Euan, *The European Reformation*, Oxford: Oxford University Press, 1991, pp. 79ff.

29. For text see Noll, Mark A. (ed.), *Confessions and Catechisms*, pp. 202–203. Purgatory had already been a matter of dispute between Eastern Orthodox and Roman Catholics at the Council of Florence in 1439: for an account of this see Hayes, Zachary, 'The Purgatorial View', in William Crockett (ed.), *Four Views on Hell*, Grand Rapids: Zondervan, 1992, pp. 111–13.

30. Eg. DiNiola, J., *The Diversity of Religions: A Christian Perspective*, Washington DC: The Catholic University Press, 1992.

31. For Augustine's development of the doctrine, and for a detailed history of purgatory, see Le Goff, J. *The Birth of Purgatory*, Trans. A. Goldhammer. Chicago: University of Chicago Press, 1984. For a comprehensive study of patristic eschatology, see Daley, *Hope*.

3:11–15. Here, Paul writes in reference to what believers 'build' on the foundation of Christ, 'If it is burned up, the builder will suffer loss; the builder, however, will be saved, but only as one escaping through the flames' (3:15). The 'flames' here were taken by Augustine and Caesarius to chasten believers after they have been judged on the last day. Protestants, however, have tended to view them as being synonymous with final judgment itself.[32]

Another key text in the historical development of the doctrine of purgatory is Matthew 12:31. Both Augustine and Gregory the Great inferred from Jesus' words here that God forgives sinners beyond death and final judgment. Gregory wrote:

> As for certain lesser faults, we must believe that, before the final judgment, there is a purifying fire (*purgatorius ignis*), for he who is the truth declares that 'whoever utters blasphemy against the Holy Spirit will not be pardoned either in this age, or in the age which is to come' (Matt.12:31). From this statement, it is to be understood that certain others will be forgiven in the age which is to come.[33]

It is a key assumption of the purgatorial view that suffering makes people whole. Purgatory is therefore seen as a purposeful experience of cleansing rather than a process of unremitting torment. By the same token, it is regarded as a stage along the path to perfection. Advocates of the doctrine routinely point out that for many people in this life, endurance of suffering can

---

32. Augustine, Exposition on Psalm 37, 3 in *Exposition on the Book of Psalms*, Peabody, Mass.: Hendrikson, 1995; Caesarius (Saint), Archbishop of Arles, *Sermons (III Vols)*, Trans. Mary Magdeleine Muller, Washington DC: Catholic University Press, 1956–1973, *Vol III*, p. 179. For a discussion of this and other texts traditionally used to defend purgatory see Hayes, 'Purgatorial View', pp. 91–118. Evangelical and liberal responses follow from John Walvoord, William Crockett and Clark Pinnock at pp. 119–34.

33. Gregory the Great, *Dialogia*, IV.xli.3, in *Sources Chretiennes, Vol. 265*. Ed. Albert de Vogue, Paris: Cerf, 1980, 148:12–18. Augustine, *City of God*, Trans. Henry Bettenson, Harmondsworth: Penguin, 1984, 21.24. See also Catherine of Genoa's influential reflections in Treatise on Purgatory, Iii, v, in da Genova, Unile Bonzi (ed.) *Edizione Critica dei Manoscritti Cateriniani*, Genoa: Marietti, pp. 327–32, n.d.

foster humility, endurance, bravery, and concentration on the good gifts of God, and suggest that it is logical to see this growth in holiness continuing beyond the grave. Alongside this argument goes the conviction that people who have not died may offer prayer and service to God so that those in purgatory may move more quickly through their chastisement. The Apocrypha contains a second century BC text, 2 Maccabees, in which the hero, Judas, prays for those who have died, thereby making 'atonement' for them, 'so that they might be delivered from their sin' (12:45, cf. 12:42, NRSV). This reference has often been used by Roman Catholic theologians to justify the practice of saying prayers, making offerings and performing masses for the dead.[34] It was also used to defend the sale of indulgences – acts of devotion made and charged at a fee by the church as a means to shortening others' time in purgatory. It was against this practice in particular that the Reformers reacted during the sixteenth century. Martin Luther's 95 Theses (1517), which are often taken as a starting-point for the Reformation, opposed indulgences on the grounds that they preyed on laypeople's fears in order to fund the institution of the church.[35]

The strength of Protestant reaction to purgatory at the Reformation can be seen in the twenty-second of the Thirty-Nine Articles of the Church of England (1563). This states that 'The Romish Doctrine concerning Purgatory, Pardons, Worshipping and Adoration, as well of Images as of Reliques, and also invocation of Saints, is a fond thing vainly invented, and grounded upon no warranty of Scripture, but rather repugnant to the Word of God.' Taking the Bible (without the Apocrypha) as a final authority, Protestants in general, and evangelical Protestants in particular, have since concurred that there is little or no Scriptural warrant for the doctrine. They have also claimed that the notion of believers needing to

---

34. Hayes, 'The Purgatorial View', pp. 104–105.

35. For the full text of the 95 theses, see Dillenberger, John (ed.), *Martin Luther: Selections from His Writings*, New York: Anchor, 1961, pp. 489–500. Zwingli also anathematised purgatory in his 67 articles (1523).

be 'purified' after death denies the effectiveness of Christ's atonement. If the death of Christ justifies believers to God once for all by redeeming them from sin and guilt, then to add another stage where this process is repeated denies the power of the cross.[36]

Universal Salvation and the Population of Heaven

Universalism holds that in the end all human beings will be saved. As such, it is primarily concerned with the doctrine of salvation (soteriology), and does not bear immediately on the nature of hell *per se*. Having said this, an obvious corollary of universalism is that hell does not exist in any objective sense – or at least that if it does, it will be empty at the end of the age. It is this corollary which is most relevant to us here, but to understand it we need to review the development and current shape of universalist theology.

The earliest universalist apologetics emerged from the Greek church fathers Clement of Alexandria (c.150–215), his pupil Origen (185–254) and Gregory of Nyssa (c.330–395). All began with the premise that since God was merciful, his punishment of sinners must be medicinal rather than endlessly punitive. So for Clement vengeance was unbecoming of God, since to wreak revenge was 'to return evil for evil, [whereas] God chastises for the benefit of the chastised'.[37] In Origen's view this chastisement could vary according to the severity of sins committed on earth, but fundamentally 'God acts in dealing with sinners as a physician, [and] the fury of his anger is profitable for the purging of souls'.[38] Likewise, Gregory

---

36. For a characteristic statement of this objection see Walvoord, John F., 'Response to Zachary J. Hayes' in William Crockett (ed.), *Four Views on Hell*, Grand Rapids: Zondervan, 1992, pp. 120–21.
37. Clement of Alexandria, *Stromateis*, VII:xvi:102. Cit. Bettenson, Henry, *The Early Christian Fathers*, Oxford University Press. 1956, p. 182.
38. Origen, *De Principiis*, II.x.4,6. Cit. Bettenson, *The Early Christian Fathers*, Oxford/New York: Oxford University Press, 1956, p. 258.

insisted that 'it is not punishment chiefly and principally that the Deity, as Judge, afflicts sinners with; but He operates ... only to get the good separated from the evil and to attract it into the communion of blessedness'.[39] The communion in question was one in which all creatures would be found 'gazing at the same goal of their desire, [with] no evil left in anyone'.[40]

These views were framed most immediately in response to gnostic assertions that only an evil deity could punish people forever. More profoundly, however, they reflected the vision of a whole cosmos being gradually reconciled or restored to its creator, a vision described by the term *apokatastasis* (restitution). As most definitively articulated by Origen, this 'consummation of all things' meant that, rather than being annihilated, the substance of the universe would change in quality such that God would be able to be 'all in all'.[41] Hence Origen's implication that even Satan could be redeemed: indeed, Origen took those passages in the New Testament which describe the 'destruction' of the devil to denote God's defeat of his 'purpose and hostile will', rather than the end of his existence.[42]

After fierce condemnation by Augustine, universalism was formally anathematised at the Second Council of Constantinople in 553, along with Origen himself.[43] It then virtually disappeared from Western theology during the Middle Ages, being advocated seriously only in the work of the Irishman John Scotus Erigena, and in the writings of certain less prominent mystics. Indebted to Augustine as they were, the great Reformers Martin Luther and John Calvin both repudiated universalism in clear terms. For Luther in particular, it represented an offence against the key principle of justification by

---

39. Gregory of Nyssa, 'Select Writings and Letters', in *Nicene and Post-Nicene Fathers V,* Oxford, 1893, p. 448.
40. Cit. Daley, *Hope*, p. 86.
41. Origen, *De Principiis*, I.vi.1–4.
42. Origen, *De Principiis*, III.vi.5.
43. Leith, John. H. (ed.), *Creeds of the Churches (Third Edition)*, Louisville: John Knox Press, 1982, p. 50.

faith alone. Without such justification by faith, he was adamant that it would be impossible for anyone to escape 'sin, death [and] hell'.[44] Inasmuch as it had located salvation in cosmic restitution rather than the victory of Christ on the cross, Origen's *apokatastasis* contrasted radically with Luther's doctrinal foundations.

Calvin's rejection of universal salvation took a somewhat different form, but the contrast was equally marked. For the French reformer it denied that biblical process of election whereby God had chosen Israel from among the nations under the Old Covenant, and had decreed in the New that only some would be chosen for everlasting bliss, with others eternally predestined to hell.[45]

On the more radical wing of the Reformation, however, universalism was more readily received. Indeed, the German Anabaptist Hans Denck (c.1495–1527) did much to revive restitutionist thinking, and even if his ideas failed to penetrate Mennonite and Hutterite theology in any decisive way, they were incorporated into the radical German pietism of Jakob Boehme (1575–1624), Johann Wilhelm Peterson (1649–1727) and Ernst Christoph Hochmann (1670–1721), leaders whose influence persists in 'left wing' German pietism to this day. Through the missionary endeavours of George de Benneville and the German Baptist Brethren, they then passed to North America, where they were most influentially propounded by the Unitarian movement.[46]

---

44. Luther, Martin, 'Preface to the New Testament', in Dillenberger, John (ed.), *Martin Luther: Selections from His Writings*, New York: Anchor Books, 1961, p. 15–17.

45. Calvin, John, *Institutes of Christian Religion*, Trans. F.L. Battles. Philadelphia: The Westminster Press, 1960, III:24:xii–xvii, pp. 978–87.

46. For more on the development of universalism in the post-Reformation and modern periods see Eller, David B., 'Universalism', in Elwell, Walter (ed.), *Evangelical Dictionary of Theology*, Exeter: Paternoster, 1984, pp. 1129–30; Hart, Trevor, 'Universalism: Two Distinct Types', in Cameron, Nigel M. de S. (ed.), *Universalism and the Doctrine of Hell*, Carlisle: Paternoster, 1992, pp. 1–34; Powys, 'Hell and Universalism'; Rowell, *Hell and the Victorians*.

In England, evangelical repudiation of universalism intensi-fied during the Wesley-Whitefield revival, when the popular preachers James Relly and John Murray were excommuni-cated from the Methodist movement for their restitutionist teaching. Later, Andrew Jukes met strong opposition when he advocated universalism in his book *The Restitution of All Things* (1867). Indeed, from the late eighteenth century onwards, universalist ideas became almost exclusively associated with liberal theologians like Jonathan Mayhew, Charles Chauncey, Hosea Ballou and Charles Skinner.[47]

Today, universalism remains a largely non-evangelical view, although there are signs that it has begun to have some influence on the more radical wing of evangelicalism. Contemporary universalism takes several different forms, but for our purposes it can be divided into three main types.[48] The first of these may be termed *pluralistic universalism*, and has been exemplified in mod-ern times by the work of Ernst Troeltsch and John Hick.[49] This conceives salvation as something that can occur 'outside' Jesus Christ, and is based on the premise that, in a world of many faiths, God must distribute his saving purpose through other religions and philosophies. The second is what we shall call *inclusivistic universalism*, and is represented variously in the work of Paul Tillich, John Macquarrie, Vernon White and Jürgen Moltmann.[50]

47. Jukes, Andrew, *The Second Death and the Restitution of All Things*, Reprinted by Scripture Studies Concern/Concordant, Hornchurch, 1976; Eller, 'Universalism', pp. 1129–30; Powys, 'Hell and Universalism'.

48. Here we are building on distinctions made by Hart, 'Universalism', pp. 1–34.

49. Troeltsch, Ernst, *The Absoluteness of Christianity and the History of Religions*, London: SCM Press 1972 [Originally published in 1901 as *The Absolute Validity of Christianity*.]; Hick, John, 'The Non-Absoluteness of Christianity', in J. Hick and P. Knitter (eds.), *The Myth of Christian Uniqueness. Toward a Pluralistic Theology of Re-ligions*, New York: Orbis, 1987; Hick, *Death and Eternal Life*; Hick, John, *Evil and the God of Love (2nd Edn.)*, London, Macmillan, 1977 [1966].

50. Tillich, Paul, *Systematic Theology*, Welwyn, Herts.: James Nisbet & Co., 1968; Macquarrie, John, *Christian Hope*, Oxford: Mowbray, 1978; White, Vernon, *Atone-ment and Incarnation*, Cambridge: Cambridge University Press, 1991; Moltmann, Jürgen, 'The Logic of Hell' in Bauckham, Richard (ed.), *God Will Be All in All: The Eschatology of Jürgen Moltmann*, Edinburgh: T&T Clark, 1999, pp. 43–7.

Arguably, it is also taught by Karl Barth.[51] This more or less accepts the uniqueness of God's revelation in Christ, but instead of demanding overt faith in him as the sole means of redemption, suggests that non-Christians may be redeemed 'unknowingly' by his grace. The third type may be dubbed *hopeful universalism*. This proposes that universal salvation is the most consistent, just and authentic inference to be drawn from the Christian Scriptures, but accepts that the population of heaven is ultimately determined by God alone. Advocates of this position include the Anglican liberal John A.T. Robinson and – more significantly for our purposes – the Dutch Reformed scholar Jan Bonda.[52] Barth could also be included under this heading, although we shall see that it may finally be best to regard his approach as *sui generis*.

While supporters of universalism may adopt distinct *theological* approaches, they tend to appeal to the same basic biblical texts.[53] Two of the most commonly-cited come from Paul's letter to the Romans:

> Consequently, just as the result of one man's trespass was condemnation for all, so also the result of one act of righteousness was justification that brings life for all. (Rom. 5:18)

> For God has bound all over to disobedience so that he may have mercy on them all. (Rom. 11:32)

---

51. Barth, Karl, *Church Dogmatics*, Trans. G.W. Bromiley & T.F. Torrance. Edinburgh: T&T Clark, 1956–1977, *II.1*, pp. 274, 373, 553; *II.2*, pp. 2, 27, 92, 164, 265, 496; *III.2*, pp. 562, 602–607, 609, 612. For a review of debate surrounding Barth's position on hell and universalism see Colwell, John, 'The Contemporaneity of Divine Decision: Reflections on Barth's Denial of "Universalism", in Cameron, Nigel de S., *Universalism and the Doctrine of Hell*, Carlisle: Paternoster, 1992, pp. 139–160. Also Bromiley, Geoffrey W., *Introduction to the Theology of Karl Barth*, Edinburgh: T&T Clark, 1979, pp. 97ff.

52. Robinson, J.A.T., *In the End, God*, London: Collins, 1968; Bonda, Jan, *The One Purpose of God: An Answer to the Doctrine of Eternal Punishment*, Grand Rapids: Eerdmans, 1998 [1993].

53. Helpful documentation is provided on this topic in Wright, N.T., 'Towards a Biblical View of Universalism', *Themelios* 4:2 (1979), 54–58.

Universalists characteristically assume from these verses that 'all' denotes the final redemption of all *individuals*. Echoing the classic evangelical response to this, however, Tom Wright notes that if we were to maintain this meaning for 'all' here, we would have to do so in the teeth of Romans 2:6–16, 14:11–12 and related passages from Paul's letters (e.g. 2 Thess. 2:7–10).[54] Certainly, it does appear that Romans 5 is dealing with comparisons of, rather than parallels with, the word 'all'. The most likely meaning would therefore appear to be: 'How much *more* then will salvation come to many through one man's act of righteousness.' The comparison here becomes not 'all ... all' or 'many ... many', but 'all ... many.'[55] Within the structure of Romans as a whole, Wright shows how Chapter 5 acts as a bridging passage between a discussion of justification by faith and an explanation of how this is experienced in the community of faith. One of the dominating themes of Romans is Paul's concentration on the difference between Jew and Gentile – or more correctly, the lack of difference. Thus Wright comments that the correct reading of 'all' in verses 12 and 18 is not 'all individually' but 'Jews and Gentiles alike'.[56]

The same concern applies to Romans 11:32. Paul is at this point demonstrating the role that Jews have to play in the church – all men and women, of whatever race, are shut up in disobedience, in order that God may have mercy on all men and women, of whatever race. Jews may still have a role, but this is conditional – '*if* they do not persist in unbelief'.

Another Pauline text regularly adduced by universalists is Philippians 2:10, with its declaration that at the sight of the glorified Christ 'every knee should bow, in heaven and on earth and under the earth'. However, while this draws a picture of all humanity coming into the presence of Christ, it cannot be taken to justify universalism, since the bowing takes place at

---

54. Wright, 'Universalism', 55.
55. See the comments of Sanders, E.P., *Paul and Palestinian Judaism*, London: SCM, 1997, p. 473.
56. Wright, 'Universalism', 56. See also Dunn, J.D.G., *Word Biblical Commentary: Romans 1–8*, Dallas: Word, 1988, p. 285.

his judgment seat. The source imagery most probably derives from Isaiah 45:23, which underlines the fact that all will kneel not because all have been saved, but because all are about to learn their ultimate fate.

Further evidence for a universalist view is commonly inferred from 1 Corinthians 15:22: 'For as in Adam all die, so in Christ will all be made alive.' Hick, for example, believes that Paul is here envisaging 'a universal fall in Adam paralleled by a universal restoration in Christ'.[57] However, the 'all' who are 'made alive' in Christ are clearly those who *already belong* to Christ (v. 23). Indeed, the assumption that those 'in Christ' could include unbelievers would be alien to Paul, as the phrase is elsewhere used strictly in connection with the redeemed (cf. Eph. 1:3,9,11).

Just as Origen's universalism was related to cosmological restoration or *apokatastasis,* more recent universalists have used texts like 1 Corinthians 15:28 and Ephesians 1:9–10 to support the 'restitution of all things':

> When Christ has [put everything under his feet] then the Son himself will be made subject to him who put everything under him, so that God may be all in all.

> And he made known to us the mystery of his will according to his good pleasure, which he purposed in Christ, to be put into effect when the times will have reached their fulfilment – to bring all things in heaven and on earth together under one head, even Christ.

Supportive of universalism as these texts might seem in isolation, they must be placed in their wider context. Indeed, 1 Corinthians 6:9 reminds us that there are those who will *not* 'inherit the kingdom of God'. The fact that God will be 'all in all' may confirm his ultimate sovereignty over the universe, but this does not necessarily imply a cosmic restoration of all human beings. In fact, we shall see in Chapter 7 that far from being *impaired* by the persistence of hell, this divine sovereignty might actually be *borne out* by it. Likewise, the Ephesians text

---

57. Hick, *Death and Eternal Life,* Basingstoke: Macmillan, 1985, p. 247.

denotes a final rule and authority that does not self-evidently exclude hell. One of the key themes of Ephesians is the division between the church and the world – a division which is linked to the fact that there *is* a wickedness on which God's wrath will come, and over which he will reign triumphant forever (cf. Eph. 3:10–11, 5:6).

In the Pastoral Epistles, Paul affirms that God 'desires everyone to be saved and to come to the knowledge of the truth' (1 Tim. 2:3,4). This appears to convey a universalist intent, but the context is one of intercession for all *levels* of society, including 'kings and all who are in high positions'. God is not restricted to one social class or group, just as he is not restricted to any one race. This is the same message as in the Romans passages cited above. Although frequently referred to in the universalist work we have cited, this statement must be reconciled with other affirmations, made within the very same letter, of future judgment and condemnation (5:24, 6:9–11). It is clearly one thing to assert that God *desires* all to be saved, but quite another to assume that this is what in fact occurs. As much as anything else, such an assumption would violate the facility God has allowed his creatures, to reject or to accept his gospel in faith.[58]

Indeed, apart from the direct charge that universalism lacks biblical warrant, this suggestion that it denigrates the place of faith in salvation is just one of a series of theological critiques commonly made by evangelicals. Further objections are that universalism trivialises sin by underplaying divine punishment; that it compromises morality by denying that good or evil choices make any ultimate difference, and that it betrays the missionary mandate of Christ by making evangelism and conversion incidental to salvation.[59]

---

58. For treatments of this crucial question of freedom in respect of universalism see Hick, *Death and Eternal Life*, Basingstoke, Macmillan, 1985, pp. 249ff., and the response of Stephen Travis: *Christian Hope and the Future of Man*, Leicester: IVP, 1980, p. 130. Also Robinson, *In the End*, pp. 99ff., and the assessment of Trevor Hart, 'Universalism', pp. 17–34.

59. For more detail on evangelical objections to universalism see Blum, Edwin, 'Shall You Not Surely Die?' *Themelios* 4:2 (1979), 58–61.

While endorsing these objections, detailed exposition of them lies beyond our scope here. Our main concern is with the constitution of hell itself. Suffice it to say that we believe that hell does exist, and that it is occupied to some degree.

Although we understand universalism to be divergent from authentic evangelical faith, we acknowledge that a small number of theologians working in evangelical contexts would disagree. The North American scholars Neal Punt and Thomas Talbott, for example, have both published 'evangelical apologetics' for universalism.[60] However, probably the most detailed study to have emerged from this marginal strand of 'evangelical universalism' in recent times is that offered by Jan Bonda.[61]

Bonda bases his soteriology on an exposition of Romans. For example, Romans 3.29–30 is used to argue that God wishes to save all people – not just those who believe, but all Jews and all Gentiles. The final salvation of Israel, which Bonda takes to include Jews who refuse the gospel, is a clear indication of God's universalistic purpose for the world as a whole. Hence the 'coming of the kingdom' in the New Testament is applied to the time when God will bring all, dead and alive, back to him. Bonda readily concedes the problems of human freedom and salvation by faith alone to which we have alluded, and is thereby led to a hopeful, rather than a dogmatic universalism.

At various points in his argument, Bonda acknowledges a debt to the work of the Swiss Reformed theologian Karl Barth. Evangelical scholars continue to debate whether or not Barth was a universalist, and whether in this sense his thinking on hell and salvation is compatible with an evangelical

---

60. Punt, Neal, *Unconditional Good News: Toward an Understanding of Biblical Universalism*, Grand Rapids: Eerdmans, 1980; Talbott, Thomas, 'The New Testament and Universal Reconciliation'. *Christian Scholar's Review* XXI:4 (1992). For a review of the main points of 'evangelical universalism' see Fudge, *Fire*, pp. 199–206.

61. Bonda, *One Purpose*.

perspective.[62] The debate is complex, but centres on an apparent tension in Barth's recasting of the Reformed doctrine of election. Barth is keen to redefine the 'double decree' proposed by John Calvin, whereby God predestines certain individuals to heaven and others to hell. Seeking to move beyond this dualistic and potentially 'arbitrary' view of election, Barth focuses not on the eternal fate of particular human persons, but on the redemptive person and work of Jesus Christ, the Saviour of the world. From the Pauline concept of our being 'in Christ', Barth construes a soteriology in which the Son himself is elected *on our behalf.* As the universal 'elected man', his election is at once both an election to damnation (as he is accursed for us on the cross) and to eternal life (as his death makes atonement for the sin of the cosmos and as he is raised to glory). By concentrating divine damnation on the cross in this way, Barth argues that what appears to be reprobation is in fact an act of 'rejecting love'. Moreover, being divine, this act is so pervasive in its effect that there is no 'hiding' from it: all are implicated in the redemption it achieves:

> For in [God's] union with this one man [Jesus Christ] He has shown His love to all and His solidarity with all. In this One He has taken upon Himself the sin and guilt of all, and therefore rescued them all by higher right from the judgment which they had rightly incurred, so that He is really the true consolation of all. In Him He is our Helper and Deliverer in the midst of death. For in the death of this One it has taken place that all we who had incurred death by our sin and guilt have been released from death as He became a Sinner and Debtor in our place, accepting the penalty and paying the debt.[63]

While this undoubtedly looks like universalism, it must be understood in terms of an ontic or 'objective' change which still calls for noetic uptake – that is, a response of faith. What is

---

62. For discussion of this debate see Colwell, 'Divine Decision', pp. 139–60. See also Bromiley, Geoffrey W., *Introduction to the Theology of Karl Barth*, Edinburgh: T&T Clark, 1979, pp. 97ff.; Berkouwer, G.C., *The Triumph of Grace in the Theology of Karl Barth*, Grand Rapids: Eerdmans, 1956, pp. 290ff; idem *Return of Christ*, Grand Rapids: Eerdmans, 1972, pp. 390; Bloesch, D.G., *Essentials of Evangelical Theology*. Vol 2. San Francisco: Harper Row, 1979, pp. 224ff.
63. *CD III.2*, p. 613.

either unclear, or so complexly wrought that it has appeared
unclear to many evangelicals, is the extent to which Barth
understands this faith-response to be decisive in *effecting*, rather
than merely *disclosing*, divine salvation for any particular
person. Given the cosmic scope of election 'in Christ', Barth is
mostly reluctant to envisage the possibility that anyone might
either reject it or be rejected from it. At certain points, however, he does appear to countenance such rejection on the
grounds that God's all-encompassing love must be a love
which liberates people to isolate themselves from His reach if
they are insistent on so doing.[64]

It may be that more theologians from the evangelical
constituency will follow Punt, Talbott and Bonda in seeking to
assimilate universalist ideas within the evangelical fold, rather
than feeling compelled to pursue them beyond it. Others will
no doubt continue to champion Barth, either as a radically
inclusive but finally non-universalist ally of evangelicalism, or
as one who offers an acceptable step towards universalism for
evangelical theology. What seems clear is that in an increasingly
multi-cultural, pluralist society, the universalism which now
underlies most forms of liberal Christianity is likely to present
an ever-greater challenge for evangelicals.

While rejecting universalism as a theological position, we
would nevertheless emphasise that God's mercy might extend
further than we can legitimately contemplate. As Wright
insists, 'it is no part of Christian duty to set bounds to God's
grace, to dictate whom God may bring to faith and whom He
may not'.[65] We shall expand on this point in Chapter 6, but
would underline here that from a biblical viewpoint, however
widely God's salvation extends, it *is* a salvation which comes by
grace through faith, rather than by right.

64. *CD III.2*, pp. 186ff.; 602–40. See discussion in Colwell, 'Divine Decision',
pp. 146–60.
65. Wright, 'Universalism', 57.

Summary

As we have prepared the ground for our main discussion, it has become clear that while evangelicals may differ on the precise details of divine condemnation, they consistently affirm certain points relevant to it. Chief among these are: the reality of death as a consequence of universal sin; the prospect of final resurrection for believers and non-believers alike, and the awesome judgment of everyone to either heaven or hell. These may seem fairly unexceptional 'lowest common denominators', but it has been necessary to establish them before we move on to examine the nature of hell itself, not least because they represent the eschatological substance of the great confessions of the early church – the Apostles' and Nicene creeds.[66]

Important though they are in themselves, however, we would emphasise that the main focus of the current debate on hell among evangelicals does not concern these 'background' issues. Rather, controversy has arisen over the duration, quality, finality and purpose of *hell itself*.[67] As we move on to address these matters in detail, we shall begin by identifying the relevant biblical data, since it is from this that evangelicals will expect, first and foremost, to discover what hell is, how long it lasts and why it exists at all.

---

66. 'Jesus Christ ... will come to judge the living and the dead'; 'I believe in ... the resurrection of the body' (Apostles' Creed); 'Jesus Christ ... will come again with glory to judge the living and the dead'; 'We look forward to the resurrection of the dead' (Nicene Creed).
67. This four-fold classification is usefully defined by Powys, 'Hell and Universalism', pp. 93–138.

3

Hell in Scripture: Identifying the Relevant Texts

The Christian doctrine of hell is ultimately a construct of systematic theology. This is to say that it represents a programmatic synthesis of all relevant material from the canon of Old and New Testament Scripture, as developed through centuries of ecclesiastical debate and reflection. We shall explore these systematic theological dimensions of hell in the next two chapters. First, however, it will be helpful simply to identify the biblical 'building blocks' from which the doctrine has developed. While realising the need for creedal and dogmatic formulations, evangelicals will judge the validity of these formulations first and foremost on their correspondence with pertinent biblical teaching. As an initial step, then, we shall here simply identify those verses that deal with hell, placing them in context.

Old Testament

The Old Testament reflects Israelite life and faith over many hundreds of years and in very different circumstances. One would therefore expect to find a variety of views expressed, particularly on issues not central to the Israelites' covenant faith. Yet in respect of death and the afterlife, there is widespread general agreement.

The Old Testament concentrates primarily on the present life, in which God reveals himself to his people and they obey, serve and worship him. Death is often mentioned as an event in the historical books, or as something dreaded in the psalms, but there is very little interest in life after death. This attitude is demonstrated clearly in Hezekiah's psalm of thanksgiving after recovery: 'For the grave [Sheol] cannot praise you, death cannot sing your praise; those who go down to the pit cannot hope for your faithfulness. The living, the living – they praise you, as I am doing today' (Is. 38:17–18).

Most Israelites probably believed that everyone who died went down to the underworld, a dark, silent place of dreary half-existence. The Old Testament contains very little description of this underworld, although Isaiah pictures the mighty king of Babylon descending there, and its inhabitants being roused to greet him: 'The grave [Sheol] below is all astir to meet you at your coming; it rouses the spirits of the departed[1] to greet you – all those who were leaders in the world ... they will say to you, "You also have become weak as we are; you have become like us" (Is. 14:9–11).' In similar vein, Ezekiel portrays a vast subterranean cavern, with separate places for different groups of fallen warriors (Ezek. 32:17–32).

Several phrases imply that the dead were expected to rejoin their ancestors. So Abraham 'breathed his last ... died ... was gathered to his people ... and [was] buried' (Gen. 25:8). So, too, Kings and Chronicles note that many rulers of Israel and Judah 'slept with their fathers'. These phrases cannot mean family burial, since Abraham was not buried in his ancestral tomb, and neither were David, Ahaz and Manasseh. Rather, they suggest some form of afterlife reunification.

Some texts seem to imply that everyone goes to the same place, whether they have been godly or ungodly in their earthly life. Thus when Saul consults the witch of Endor, the spirit of the dead Samuel comes *up* from

---

1. Or 'shades' (RSV). The term (*repha'im*) occurs 8 times in the Old Testament. Its precise meaning is obscure.

the ground.[2] This suggests that Samuel was in the under-world. This underworld is usually referred to by the Hebrew name Sheol,[3] and is occasionally called the pit, or destruction.[4] The use of these terms is significant for a number of reasons:

i)   They occur only about 100 times, which is very little given the length of the Old Testament and the importance it attaches to death as an event and a concept. This underlines the point that the focus of Israel's faith was the present life rather than life beyond the grave.

ii)   The terms occur mostly in the Psalms, prophets and wisdom literature. They also occur a few times in narrative, mostly in direct speech.[5] As such, they are terms of personal emotion rather than of factual record.

iii)   They are used mostly to describe human fate, not simply to speculate about the afterlife.[6] On all these points the Old Testament differs notably from its religious and cultural environment.

iv)   Most significantly of all, these terms refer mainly to the fate which the wicked should receive, and which the righteous wish to

---

2. The text of 1 Sam. 28 assumes this really is Samuel, not a demonic apparition as is sometimes suggested.

3. The NIV usually translates Sheol as 'the grave'; cf. Harris, R.L., 'Why Hebrew *She'ol* was translated "grave"', in K.L. Barker (ed.), *The Making of a Contemporary Translation*, London: Hodder & Stoughton, 1987, pp. 75–92. Idem, 'The meaning of the Word Sheol as Shown by Parallels in Poetic Texts', *Bulletin of the Evangelical Theological Society* 4 (1961), 129–35; idem 'she'ol', in R.L. Harris, G.L. Archer & B.K. Waltke (eds.), *Theological Wordbook of the Old Testament*, Chicago: Moody, 1980, pp. 892f. While this translation would overcome the apparent difficulty of the wicked and the righteous going to the same place, it is unlikely for several reasons: (i) Is. 14 does not describe the grave. (ii) Sheol is often pictured as the lowest imaginable point, in contrast to the highest heavens. The NIV is sometimes forced to acknowledge this in translation, e.g. 'depths of the grave' (Am. 9:2); 'realm of death' (Deut. 32:22).

4. Sheol 65 (or 66) times; 'pit' (*bor, be'er, shahat*) 36 times; destruction (*'abaddon*) 6 times.

5. E.g. occurrence of Sheol: psalms: 21, prophets: 17, wisdom etc: 20, narrative: 8. The one exception where Sheol occurs in narrative discourse is actually an echo of direct speech, Num. 16:30,33.

6. E.g. for Sheol, 34 texts of descent to Sheol, 7 of deliverance or avoidance – i.e. nearly two-thirds. For further detail on these points, see Johnston, P.S., ' "Left in Hell"? Psalm 16, Sheol and the Holy One', in P.E. Satterthwaite *et al.* (eds.), *The Lord's Anointed: Interpretation of Old Testament Messianic Texts*, Carlisle: Paternoster, pp. 213–222; Powys, *Hard Question*, pp. 65–106.

escape.[7] Many scholars think that the righteous simply wanted to avoid immediate, untimely death, but accepted that they would eventually go to Sheol. However, this is questionable. Several godly people talk as if they are headed for Sheol, but only in their extreme desperation.[8] Jacob, for instance, speaks of going to Sheol when he thinks that Joseph is dead and that he will lose Benjamin. But later, after he is happily reunited with his favourite sons, his death is described in several ways, and none of these mentions Sheol.[9] Two texts imply that everyone goes to Sheol, but these occur in contexts of divine judgment (Ps. 89:48) and of human futility (Ecc. 9:10). This predominant Old Testament use of Sheol and its synonyms to describe the fate of the wicked suggests that such terms represented the negative, unwelcome aspect of the underworld. Even so, it is important for current debates about hell to note that the underworld is never explicitly portrayed in the Old Testament as a place of judgment, punishment or torture. While psalmists often want the wicked to go there, the fate they have in mind is death itself, rather than any specific form of afterlife.

Very occasionally, an alternative to the underworld is suggested. Two Old Testament characters, for instance, avoided death: 'God took Enoch away' and 'Elijah went up to heaven in a whirlwind' (Gen. 5:24, 2 Kings 2:11). But these events never function as exemplary models for psalmists, prophets or sages. A few psalmists are so excited by their present communion with God that they believe it will continue after death in some unspecified form (Ps. 16:10, 49:15 [contrast v. 7], 73:24). This, however, is a step of faith, and no further details are given. Besides, these texts are exceptions. Most other psalmists who mention death expect it to be the end.

Two Old Testament passages refer clearly to resurrection: Isaiah 26:19 (cf. v. 14) and Daniel 12:2. Of these, only the latter mentions a resurrection of both the righteous and unrighteous to separate fates:

---

7. The ungodly are consigned to Sheol 25 times. Hence the AV often translated Sheol as 'hell'.
8. 7 times: Gen. 37:35, 42:38, 44:29, 31 (all Jacob); Is. 38:10; Job 17:13–16; Ps. 88:3.
9. Gen. 47:30, 48:21, 49:29,33.

> Multitudes who sleep in the dust of the earth will awake, some to everlasting
> life, others to shame and everlasting contempt.

The Hebrew word here translated 'everlasting' (ʿôlam)
normally indicates either the ancient past or the limitless
future. In any case, Daniel 12 does not expound the fate of
'shame and contempt' any further.

In Isaiah 66:24 all humanity will come to the restored Jerusalem and bow before the Lord:

> And they will go out and look upon the dead bodies of those who rebelled
> against me; their worm will not die, nor will their fire be quenched, and they
> will be loathsome to the whole human race.

The emphasis of this passage is on God's ultimate vindication,
as witnessed by Israel and many others. Reference to corpses
suggests recent dead who remain unburied, as in other visions
of the valley(s) around Jerusalem filled with corpses (e.g. Jer.
7:32). The dominant sense is of life degraded and terminated,
and the undying worm and unquenched fire are probably
meant to evoke this rather than any sort of conscious pain after
death.

Intertestamental Literature

Jewish thinking about life after death developed considerably
in the period between the testaments, and this is reflected in
much intertestamental literature. While this literature has
never been accepted by evangelicals as inspired or authoritative, it provides important religious and linguistic background
to the New Testament.[10] At the same time, there are two
significant difficulties. First, intertestamental texts display a
considerable variety of views, particularly with respect to life
after death. This is reflected in the opposite positions taken by

---

10. Similarly, the works of Shakespeare help us to understand some of the vocabulary of the Authorised Version of the Bible.

Sadducees and Pharisees on the resurrection (Acts 23:8). Secondly, these texts are often hard to date. Some material previously thought to be pre-Christian, and therefore a possible influence on Christian ideas, is now thought to be later and itself influenced by Christian writers.[11]

One particularly important source is 1 Enoch, written from the third century BC onwards but, like much early Jewish literature, attributed to an ancient biblical figure.[12] This develops the brief reference to 'the sons of God' (fallen angels) at Genesis 6:2 into several detailed accounts of God's dealing with the world. Enoch is shown the dead divided into four different groups awaiting judgment (ch.22).[13] The really wicked will be punished with torment for ever (23:11), as an eternal spectacle for the righteous (27:3). But elsewhere 'those who walk in the path of iniquity will be *destroyed* for ever' (91:19, our emphasis). These dual themes, of eternal torment on the one hand and eternal destruction on the other, seem to be echoed in the New Testament.

New Testament

While the New Testament shows some continuity with earlier views on life after death, it is also significantly different. This is

---

11. For good orientation to this literature, see Bauckham, R.: 'Early Jewish Visions of Hell', *Journal of Theological Studies* 41.2, (1990), 357–85; 'Descent to the Underworld', *ABD* (1992) 2:145–59; 'Life, Death and the Afterlife in Second Temple Judaism', in R.N. Longenecker (ed.), *Life in the Face of Death: The Resurrection Message of the New Testament*, Grand Rapids: Eerdmans, 1998, pp. 80–95.

12. This seems to consist of five separate books attributed to Enoch, which were later brought together. One section, the Parables or Similitudes (chs. 36–71) is often thought to betray Christian influence. The influence of 1 Enoch is seen particularly in 2 Peter (e.g. 2:4) and Jude.

13. This is the only text which categorises the dead in a fourfold way. Elsewhere there are only two categories. See Bauckham, R., 'Visiting the Places of the Dead in the Extra-Canonical Apocalypses', *Proceedings of the Irish Biblical Association*, 18, 1995, 84.

noted and explained in 2 Tim. 1:10: 'Our Saviour Jesus Christ
has destroyed death and brought life and immortality to light
through the gospel'. Here Paul focuses on the transformed
existence of believers. But Christ's teaching and work also
brought new revelation on the destiny of unbelievers, and on
the cosmos as a whole.

Matthew, Mark, Luke

Of the synoptic gospels, Matthew clearly has the most references to hell. Mark's one passage and Luke's several references
are all included in Matthew, with the exception of the parable
of the rich man and Lazarus in Luke 16. But each gospel has
one passage that features strongly in discussion of the traditional view of hell. These are:

- Matthew 25:31–46: the parable of the sheep and the
  goats, departing respectively to eternal life and eternal
  punishment
- Mark 9:43–48: Jesus' instruction to avoid hell (Gehenna)
  at all costs
- Luke 16:19–31: the parable of the rich man tormented in
  Hades, and of Lazarus in Abraham's bosom

We shall see in the next three chapters that these key words and
images have been the focus of dispute on the doctrine of hell
down the centuries (see Table, p44–5). Here, we shall make
brief introductory comments on them before assessing the history of their interpretation, and their relevance to the contemporary evangelical debate. We begin with two particularly
important terms: Gehenna and Hades.

Gehenna takes its name from the Hebrew 'Valley of
Hinnom' (*ge'hinnom*), just south of Jerusalem. This was a
notorious site of idolatry, where Ahaz and Manasseh sacrificed
their sons by fire to Molech, a god of the dead. Isaiah uses this
imagery to prophesy a funerary pyre there for the invading
king of Assyria (Is. 30:33). Josiah defiled its pagan altars in his

reform, 2 Kings 23:10, but this reform was short-lived. It was the place where dead bodies and ashes were thrown (Jer. 31:40). Reference to ashes may indicate a rubbish heap, though there is no biblical or other early reference to this.[14] Jeremiah prophesied that there would be so many dead there when Jerusalem was captured that it would be renamed the Valley of Slaughter (Jer. 7:32). Isaiah 66:24 pictures Israelites and visitors in a restored Jerusalem going out (presumably to the surrounding valley, though *ge'hinnom* is not mentioned) to gaze at the dead bodies of the Lord's enemies, with their 'undying worm' and 'unquenched fire'.

The association of fire, judgment and death with *ge'hinnom* led to the concept of a place of punishment after death, called *géenna* in Greek (Gehenna in Latin). This term occurs first in the New Testament (12 times), and then in various Jewish and Christian writings. In the New Testament it occurs mostly in the Synoptic Gospels, where it is found always on the lips of Jesus, and in four contexts:

a) Specified sin leads to Gehenna (Matt. 5:22).

b) It is better to enter life maimed than to go whole-bodied to Gehenna (Matt. 5:29, 30; Mark 9:43, 45, 47). The last reference is followed by the quote from Isaiah 66:24.

c) Jesus' followers should fear the One 'who can destroy both body and soul in Gehenna' (Matt. 10:28), or who, 'after killing the body, has the power to throw you into Gehenna' (Luke 12:5).

d) Some Pharisees were already condemned to Gehenna, and made their converts 'sons of Gehenna' (Matt. 23:15, 33).

The only other New Testament use of this term is in James 3:6, where the tongue is said to be set on fire by Gehenna.

None of the above verses specifically mentions the *duration* of Gehenna; neither do they specify its function in terms of

---

14. Cf. Head, Peter, 'The Duration of Divine Judgment in the New Testament', in K.E. Brower and M.W. Elliott (eds.), *'The Reader Must Understand': Eschatology in Bible and Theology*, Leicester: IVP, 1997, p. 223. Later rabbinic sources mention the smouldering rubbish heap.

Matthew	Mark & Luke	Text
Mt 3:7,12	Lk 3:7,17	Who warned you to flee from the coming wrath? he will burn up the chaff with unquenchable fire
Mt 5:22		anyone who says 'You fool!' will be in danger of the fire of hell
Mt 5:29,30 18:8,9	Mk 9:43, 45,47	your whole body to go / be thrown into hell / fire of hell / eternal fire
	Mk 9:48	where their worm does not die and the fire is not quenched
Mt 7:13		the road that leads to destruction
Mt 8:12 22:13 25:30 24:51	Lk 13:28	thrown outside, into the darkness, where there will be weeping and gnashing of teeth a place with the hypocrites, where there will be ...
Mt 10:15 11:23 11:24	Lk 10:12 10:14 10:15	more bearable for Sodom and Gomorrah on the day of judgment more bearable for Tyre and Sidon ... Capernaum ... will go down to Hades
Mt 10:28		Be afraid of the one who can destroy both body and soul in hell
	Lk 12:5	Fear him who ... has the power to throw you into hell
Mt 12:41 12:42	Lk 11:32 11:31	The men of Nineveh will stand up at the judgment The Queen of the South will rise at the judgment
Mt 13:42 13:50		thrown into the fiery furnace, where there will be weeping and gnashing of teeth
Mt 16:18		the gates of Hades will not overcome it
Mt 23:15 23:33		make him twice as much a son of hell as you are How will you escape being condemned to hell?
Mt 25:41 25:46		into the eternal fire, prepared for the Devil and his angels they will go away to eternal punishment
	Lk 16:23, 24,28	In Hades ... in torment ... in agony in this fire ... place of torment

Concepts and Images	Context
wrath unquenchable fire	John the Baptist's teaching
fire, Gehenna	Jesus' teaching
fire, Gehenna, eternal fire .. .. .. undying worm, unquenched fire	Jesus' teaching
destruction	Jesus' teaching
darkness, weeping, gnashing of teeth darkness, weeping, gnashing of teeth darkness, weeping, gnashing of teeth weeping, gnashing of teeth	Parable: great feast Parable: wedding banquet Parable: lazy servant Parable: wicked servant
judgment .. .. Hades	Jesus' teaching
destroy, Gehenna Gehenna	Satan
judgment judgment	Jesus' teaching
fire, weeping, gnashing of teeth fire, weeping, gnashing of teeth	Parable: wheat & tares Parable: net
Hades	Peter's faith
Gehenna condemned, Gehenna	Pharisees
eternal fire eternal punishment	Parable: sheep & goats
Hades, torment, agony, fire	Story: rich man & Lazarus

punishment. In Mark 9:43–48 the ascription of 'life' to the obedient may imply its opposite – namely, death for the sinful. Conversely, the quote from Isaiah 66 may imply continued existence in hell. In Matthew 10:28, Jesus' warning about the destruction of body and soul 'in Gehenna' may imply cessation of existence.

Hades was the common Greek term for the world of the dead – a place to which everyone went. It was used to translate Sheol in the pre-Christian Greek version of the Old Testament (the Septuagint, or LXX), and in early Jewish texts written in Greek. Many scholars suggest that in New Testament times it was thought to contain all the dead, perhaps in separate sections (as in 1 Enoch). It is used 11 times in the New Testament. These usages occur in the gospels in three different contexts (two of which imply a place of punishment), and in three other contexts:

a)   Unbelieving Capernaum will be brought down to Hades (Matt. 11:24, Lk. 10:15).

b)   The gates of Hades will not overcome Christ's church (Matt. 17:18).[15]

c)   The rich man is in Hades, in torment (Lk. 16:23). He can see the poor man far away at Abraham's side, separated by a great chasm. Whether this is a different compartment of Hades or somewhere else is not stated.

d)   In Acts 2:27 and 31 Peter quotes Psalm 16:10 to argue for Jesus' resurrection. 'Sheol' here becomes 'Hades'.

e)   In 1 Corinthians 15:55 Paul quotes Hosea 13:14 to argue that death has lost its sting.[16]

f)   In Revelation 1:18, 6:8, 20:1, 14 Hades is consistently coupled with death. The risen Christ has its keys; it goes out to kill; it gives up its dead, and is finally thrown into the lake of fire.

---

15. Sheol was pictured with gates and bars (Is. 38:10, Jon. 2:7), as was the underworld in Mesopotamia.

16. Only some New Testament manuscripts have 'Hades' here.

In addition to Gehenna and Hades, further images are used to depict the realm and fate of the damned. Mention of fire is especially frequent in this regard. It is defined as 'unquench-able' by John the Baptist (Matt. 3:12), and also by Jesus as he quotes from Isaiah 66 in Mark 9:48. Likewise, it is described as 'eternal' (Greek *aiōnios*) in Jesus' parable of the sheep and the goats (Matt. 25:31–46). This parable is the only point in the gospels where 'eternal' is used in relation to the fate of the unrighteous.

Other descriptions of hell are specific to Jesus' parables: darkness, weeping and gnashing of teeth in the parables of the great feast, the wedding banquet and the lazy servant, and weeping and gnashing of teeth only in the parable of the wicked servant.

John's Gospel and Letters

John's gospel and letters differ noticeably from the synoptic gospels in that they contain no reference to Gehenna, Hades, torment, fire, etc. Instead, they portray unbelief in terms of 'perishing', 'death' and 'condemnation/judgment',[17] and belief in terms of 'salvation' and 'life'. The precise meaning of these latter concepts, and of the 'resurrection of judgment' in John 5:29, remains a matter of exegetical debate. Relevant texts are:

John 3:16	Believers 'will not perish but have eternal life'.
John 5:24	Believers 'have eternal life and will not be judged; they have crossed over from death to life'.
John 5:29	Those who have done good will 'rise to live', while those who have done evil will 'rise to be condemned'.
John 10:28	Jesus' followers (his 'sheep') will 'never perish'.
John 11:26	Believers 'will never die'.

---

17. The same Greek stem, *krinō*, is translated in the NIV as 'to judge' and 'to condemn', e.g. 5:22 (judges, judgment), 24, 29 (condemned); similarly 12:47–48.

1 John 3:14	Believers have 'passed from death to life'. Anyone who does not love 'remains in death'.
1 John 4:17 –18	Believers will have 'confidence on the day of judgment'. Fear 'has to do with punishment'.
1 John 5:16	There is a sin 'that leads to death'.

Acts

Acts similarly contains no references to hell. Resurrection and salvation are central to the apostles' preaching, but not hell. Divine judgment is sometimes mentioned, but what follows this is not specified. The relevant texts are:

2:24	God freed Jesus from death.
10:42	God appointed Jesus as 'judge of the living and the dead'.
11:18	God has given even Gentiles 'repentance unto life'.
24:25	Paul discoursed on 'the judgment to come'.

Paul's Letters

Paul also never speaks specifically of hell. He does, however, frequently deal with a number of closely related issues. Death (*thanatos*) is depicted as 'the wages of sin' at Romans 6:23, while 1 Corinthians 15:26 describes it as 'the last enemy to be destroyed' (cf. Rom. 5:12, 14:1, 1 Cor. 15:21). Divine wrath (*orgē*) is said to be in prospect for those who 'follow evil' (Rom. 2:7–9), and likewise the reprobate are described as 'objects' of God's wrath (Rom. 9:22, cf. Rom. 1:18, 2:5,8, 3:5, 4:15, 5:9, 12:19, 13:4,5; Eph. 2:3, 5:6; Col. 3:6; 1 Thess. 1:10, 2:16, 5:9). Paul insists with respect to our final reckoning (*katakrima*) that 'we must all appear before the judgment seat of Christ' (cf. Rom. 2:2,3,5,16, 3:6, 5:16, 14:10; 1 Cor. 5:13; 1Thess. 4:6; 2 Thess. 1:5; 1 Tim. 5:24; 2 Tim. 4:1). Those bound for condemnation are 'perishing' (*apollymi*) (Rom. 2:12; 1 Cor. 1:18, 15:18; 2 Cor. 2:15, 4:3; 2 Thess. 2:10) and are headed for 'destruction' (*apōleia*) (Rom. 9:22; Phil. 1:28, 3:19; 1 Thess. 5:3; 2 Thess. 1:9).

Despite this range of imagery, Paul depicts what *follows* judgment in explicit terms only at 2 Thessalonians 1:9, where sinners are said to be destined for 'eternal destruction'. Furthermore, he writes of fire only in reference to testing the work of believers (1 Cor. 3:13). Moreover, he uses *aiōnios* ('eternal') frequently to describe the life of Christian disciples, but applies it only once to the unrighteous – again, in 2 Thessalonians 1:9:

> They will be punished with everlasting destruction and shut out from the presence of the Lord and from the majesty of his power on the day he comes to be glorified in his holy people and to be marvelled at among all those who have believed.

Other Letters

Hebrews has one reference to the fate of God's enemies after judgment, speaking of 'a raging fire that will consume them' (10:27). Elsewhere in the same letter judgment itself is described as 'eternal' (6:2). James uses the terms 'destroy' and 'death' (Jas. 1:15; 4:12). 1 Peter speaks only of 'judgment' (1 Pet. 4:17), while 2 Peter also talks of 'destruction', and 'perishing' (2 Pet. 2:9; 3:7,9,16). 2 Pet. 2:9 could refer to punishment and suffering either *before* final judgment (NIV text) or *following* judgment (NIV footnote).[18] Jude mentions 'eternal fire' as a punishment for immorality (v. 7), and warns that 'blackest darkness' has been reserved 'for ever' for those 'godless people' who have infiltrated the community to which he is writing:

Heb. 6:1   Repentance is from 'acts which lead to death' (or literally, 'acts of death').

Heb. 6:2   Judgment is 'eternal'.

Heb. 10:27   Deliberate and continual sinning leads to a 'fearful expectation of judgment and of raging fire that will consume the enemies of God'.

---

18. Both views can be argued from the immediate grammar and from other New Testament and early Jewish texts. For full discussion, see Bauckham, R. J., *Jude, 2 Peter*, Waco: Word, 1983, pp. 253f.

Heb.10:39	Believers are 'not of those who shrink back and are destroyed'.
Jas. 4:12	Christ is the unique 'Lawgiver and Judge, who is able to save and destroy'.
Jas. 5:20	Whoever turns a sinner from the error of his way 'will save him from death'.
1 Pet. 4:5	Pagans will have to give account 'to him who is ready to judge the living and the dead'.
2 Pet. 2:1,3	False prophets bring 'swift destruction' on themselves. This destruction 'has not been sleeping'.
2 Pet. 2:9	The Lord knows how 'to hold the unrighteous for the day of judgment, while continuing their punishment' (NIV footnote: *or* 'for punishment until the day of judgment').
2 Pet. 2:12	False teachers will 'perish like beasts'.
2 Pet. 3:7	The present heavens and earth are being 'kept for the day of judgment and destruction of ungodly men'.
2 Pet.3:9	God does not want anyone 'to perish'.
2 Pet. 3:16	Ignorant and unstable people distort Paul's teaching 'to their own destruction'.
Jude 7	Sodom and Gomorrah . . . serve as an example of those who suffer 'the punishment of eternal fire'.
Jude 13	Godless men infiltrating the community of Jude's readers have the 'blackest darkness' reserved for them 'for ever'.
Jude 23	Disciples must 'snatch others from the fire'.

Revelation

Revelation is expressly about the future: 'what must soon take place' (1:1). Those who refuse to worship God and the Lamb will meet the 'second death' in a fiery lake of burning sulphur. There worshippers of the beast will be tormented, with smoke rising forever, and the devil, beast and false prophet will be tormented forever. Elsewhere in Revelation, God's opponents are said to face destruction, and/or exclusion from his presence:

2:11	Those who overcome will not be hurt at all by 'the second death'.
11:18	The time has come 'for destroying those who destroy the earth'.
14:9–11	Anyone worshipping the beast will be 'tormented with burning sulphur in the presence of the holy angels and of the Lamb. And the smoke of their torment [will rise] for ever and ever'.
20:6	The 'second death' has 'no power' over those who have a part in the 'first resurrection'.
20:10	The devil 'was thrown into the lake of burning sulphur, where the beast and the false prophet had been thrown. They will be tormented day and night for ever and ever.'
20:14	John sees death and Hades 'thrown into the lake of fire'. This lake of fire constitutes 'the second death'. If anyone's name is not found written in the book of life, he is also 'thrown into the lake of fire'.
21:8	Various wrongdoers have their place 'in the fiery lake of burning sulphur'. This is 'the second death'.
22:15	Everyone who loves and practises falsehood is found 'outside' the new Jerusalem.

Summary

The Old Testament largely implies a common fate of death and the gloomy underworld for all, although the way underworld terms are used suggests that it is an unwelcome destiny. A few texts indicate an alternative fate for the righteous, though without detail. Two passages mention resurrection, and Daniel 12:2 contrasts everlasting life with everlasting contempt. In the period between the testaments various views developed, including the subdivision of Sheol/Hades into separate compartments. The New Testament portrays the final fate of the unrighteous in various ways. Matthew, Mark, Luke, Jude and Revelation refer mainly to Gehenna, Hades and fire, and imply some duration of punishment. John, Paul and the other letters refer mainly to perishing, destruction and death.

This variation in biblical imagery stands behind much of the debate between traditionalists and conditionalists. Few doubt that Scripture deploys a range of images to depict the fate of unbelievers. Yet because theologians typically try to systematise biblical teaching, this range of images has been regularised into one doctrinal position or another. This process has been very apparent among evangelicals, who have deemed the eternal conscious punishment of sinners to be logically at odds with their extinction, and who have consequently disagreed on which motifs should be determinative. It is to this problem, and the qualifications and complexities attendant upon it, that we must now turn.

4

Traditionalism and Conditionalism in Church History

We have introduced the evangelical debate about hell as a debate between 'traditionalists' and 'conditionalists'. In this chapter, we shall trace the roots of the debate and chart the basic sources of division between these two groups. In the next chapter, it will become clear that more recent developments in the debate require a more nuanced classification of the positions adopted by different contributors to it.

The Traditional View: Eternal Conscious Punishment

One of the earliest surviving accounts of the view that unbelievers will suffer eternal conscious punishment in hell can be found in the writings of the North African church father Tertullian (c.160–220). In his treatise *On the Resurrection of the Flesh*, Tertullian opposes those who take the biblical language of destruction in Matthew 10:28 to imply final annihilation rather than penal treatment. Instead, he insists that 'the fire of hell is eternal – expressly announced as an everlasting penalty'. As such, it represents a 'never-ending killing' – a killing whose effect is 'more formidable than a merely human murder, which

1. Roberts & Donaldson, *Ante-Nicene Fathers*, 3:570.

is only temporal'.[1] Tertullian further develops his argument by suggesting that the conditionalist position makes the final resurrection redundant:

> It would be most absurd if the flesh should be raised up and destined to 'the killing of hell', in order to be put an end to, when it might suffer such an annihilation (more directly) if not raised again at all. A pretty paradox, to be sure, that an essence must be refitted with life, in order that it may receive that annihilation which has in fact already accrued to it![2]

Elsewhere, in his *Apology*, Tertullian declares that 'the worshippers of God will be with God for ever . . . but the profane and all who are not wholly devoted to God [will be] in the punishment of fire which is just as eternal'.[3] The parallel between eternal bliss and eternal reprobation here doubtless owes something to Tertullian's reading of Matthew 25:46. It is also likely, however, that he was influenced by the prevailing Platonic belief in the immortality of the soul.[4] Whether this concept of an 'immortal soul' was also assumed in Scripture would become a major bone of contention in ensuing debate.[5]

Another early church father who made much of the apparent symmetry between everlasting joy for the righteous and everlasting torment for the wicked was Lactantius (c.240–320). Writing of those who have 'worshipped the work of their own hands, who have either been ignorant of, or who have denied the Lord and Parent of the world', Lactantius declared: 'Their Lord [Satan] with his servants shall be seized and condemned to punishment, together with all the band of the wicked, [who] in accordance with their deeds, shall be burnt forever with perpetual fire in the sight of angels and the righteous.'[6] A very similar picture was presented by Basil of Caesarea (c.330–79), who denounced

2. Roberts & Donaldson, *Ante-Nicene Fathers*, 3:570.
3. Roberts & Donaldson, *Ante-Nicene Fathers*, 3:570.
4. Fudge, *Fire*, pp. 336–8
5. This point is discussed in the next chapter.
6. Lactantius, *The Divine Institutes*, 7:26.

any notion of a time-limit on suffering in hell as 'the devil's trickery',[7] and by Jerome (c.342–420), who taught that there would be 'eternal torments for . . . all deniers of God and the impious'.[8] Likewise, Cyril of Jerusalem (c.315–86) declared: 'If a man is a sinner, he shall receive an eternal body, fitted to endure the pains of sins, that it may burn eternally in fire, nor ever be consumed.'[9]

John Chrysostom (c.347–407) shared this eternal view of hell's pains, repudiating those who suggested 'that hell is not so terrible as it is said to be'.[10] More distinctively, he emphasised the necessity of everlasting torment as a corollary of divine justice. A renowned preacher of great oratorical skill, Chrysostom would often portray hell in vivid terms, as an encouragement to his hearers to repent and so escape God's impending wrath:

> There will be no one who can resist, no one who can escape; Christ's gentle, peaceful face will be nowhere to be seen. But as those sentenced to work in the mines are given over to rough men and no more see their families, but only their taskmasters, so it will be there – or not simply so, but much worse. For here one can appeal to the Emperor for clemency, and have the prisoner released – but there, never! They will not be released, but will remain, roasting and in such agony as cannot be expressed.[11]

Of all the early church fathers, however, the most significant advocate of eternal punishment was Augustine of Hippo (354–430). In particular, Book 21 of Augustine's *City of God* dealt extensively with the fate of unbelievers. Asserting the

---

7. Basil of Caesarea, *Regulae Brevius Tractatae*, 267. Cit. Bettenson, Henry (ed.), *The Later Christian Fathers*, Oxford/New York: Oxford University Press, 1970, p. 92.

8. Jerome, *In Isa.* 66.24. Cit. Bettenson, Henry (ed.), *The Later Christian Fathers*, Oxford/New York: Oxford University Press, p. 190.

9. Cyril of Jerusalem, 'Catechetical Lecture', XVIII, v. 19, in *Catechetical Lectures (Catechesis)*, Trans. Leo P. McCauley & Anthony A. Stephenson, Washington DC: Catholic University of America Press, 1969–1970.

10. John Chrysostom, *Homilies on the First Epistle of St. Paul to the Corinthians*, I:3; 23. Oxford: Library of the Fathers, 1839.

11. Cit. Daley, *Hope*, p. 107.

absolute sovereignty of God over both Christians and non-Christians alike, Augustine drew heavily on texts such as Mark 9:48 and Matthew 25:46 to forge what would become a familiar link between the eternity of life in Christ and the eternity of hell for those who reject the gospel:

> How absurd it is to interpret eternal punishment as meaning merely a fire of long duration while believing eternal life to signify life without end . . . The phrases are parallel: eternal punishment; eternal life. To say, in the same context, 'Eternal life will be without end, eternal punishment will have an end', is utterly ridiculous. Hence, since the eternal life of the saints will be without end, the eternal punishment of those who incur it will without doubt be endless.[12]

Importantly, Augustine went on to defend this view against certain more subtle objections which had by this point begun to find favour both outside and inside the Church. For example, he answered the point that an eternal punishment is unjustly disproportionate to any crime which could be committed in the finite context of life on earth. He did this by focussing not on specific individual misdemeanours, but on the complicity of all human beings in the universal sin of Adam. Adam's rebellion against God 'merited eternal evil, in that he destroyed in himself a good that might have been eternal'. Thus, for Augustine, once we have grasped the true enormity of what happened in Eden, and its implications for us, it is not only possible, but logical, to accept the righteousness of everlasting torment.[13]

Augustine also rebutted the Platonic idea that all punishments must be purgatorial rather than punitive. Since punishment can simply harden offenders rather than cure them, those who had decisively rejected the love of God before death might quite conceivably be immune to correction after it. In any case, Augustine insisted that neither temporal nor eternal punishments can finally be reckoned according to our

---

12. Augustine, *City of God*, XXI:23., pp. 1000–2.
13. *City of God*, XXI:12, p. 988–9.

own gradation of sin; rather, they are 'imposed on each person in accordance with the treatment he is to receive from God's providence'.[14]

Augustine's most vehement criticisms were directed against universalism, and most particularly the universalism of Origen. Emphasising that Origen's doctrine of *apokatastasis* had finally to extend to the restitution of Satan and his angels, Augustine vilified it for thus presuming to 'oppose God's words with what purports to be a higher form of compassion'.[15] More basically, he contended that it also flies in the face of Matthew 25:41, where the devil and his legions are said to be destined for 'eternal fire', and Revelation 20:10, which portrays the devil, the beast and the false prophet being tortured 'day and night for ever and ever'. Moreover, he underlined the fact that the fate of Satan's hordes is closely related to the fate of unrepentant sinners by Jesus in Matthew 25:41, such that everlasting punishment awaits them all alike.[16]

Augustine's thought had a major influence on medieval Western theology, and not least on that of the thirteenth century theologian Thomas Aquinas. It also significantly informed the mainline Protestant Reformers.

In his *Summa Contra Gentiles*, Aquinas dismissed 'the error of those who say that the punishments of the wicked are to be ended at some time', identifying it (as Augustine had done) with the extra-biblical view that all post–mortem punishment must be remedial.[17] Furthermore, while he accepted that punishments might ordinarily be proportional to the gravity of crimes committed, he constructed a simple case for eternal retribution where sin against God was concerned. This was based on the infinite nature of God himself:

---

14. *City of God*, XXI:13, p. 990.
15. *City of God*, XXI:17, p. 995.
16. *City of God*, XXI:23, pp. 1000–2.
17. *On the Truth of the Catholic Faith, Summa Contra Gentiles*, Trans. Vernon J. Bourke, Garden City, NJ.: Doubleday, 1956. Book 3, Providence, Part 2, 216 (144:8).

> The magnitude of the punishment matches the magnitude of the sin ... Now that a sin against God is infinite; the higher the person against whom the sin is committed, the graver the sin – it is more criminal to strike a head of state than a private citizen – and God is of infinite greatness. Therefore an infinite punishment is deserved for a sin committed against him.[18]

Alongside this approach to retribution, Aquinas emphasised that the suffering endured by the wicked would entail both a psychological aspect ('the pain of loss') and a physical aspect ('the pain of sense'). Hence, 'those who sin against God are not only to be punished by their exclusion from perpetual happiness, but also by the experience of something painful'.[19] This distinction played a notable part in the formation of Martin Luther's thinking on death, judgment and hell, and has become even more crucial in the modern period.

Whereas Aquinas had argued for a *balance* of spiritual and bodily suffering, Luther highlighted the former, commenting in relation to Hebrews 5:7 that 'hell is not hell because punishment is there, but because praise of God is not there'.[20] Likewise, although he remained very much committed to the unending nature of divine punishment,[21] he saw this most obviously in terms of mental torments like 'fear, terror, horror, the desire to flee, and despair'.[22]

John Calvin's emphases were similar to Luther's. At one point in his *Institutes of the Christian Religion*, he even described the Bible's images of darkness, weeping, gnashing teeth, unquenchable fire and an undying worm as 'figurative expressions' and 'metaphors' of a deeper relational separation of unbelievers from their Maker – their severance 'from all

---

18. *Summa Theologiae*, Blackfriars. New York: McGraw-Hill, 1974. Ia2ae. 27.

19. *On the Truth of the Catholic Faith, Summa Contra Gentiles*, 217.

20. Luther, Martin, 'Lectures on Titus, Philemon and Hebrews', *Luther's Works*, 29. Missouri: Concordia, 1968, pp. 176–7.

21. See e.g. Augsburg Confession, 17, which anathematises those 'who think that to condemned men and devils there shall be an end of torments'.

22. Luther, Martin, *Luther's Works: Career of the Reformer I*. Ed. H.J. Grimm, *Luther's Works*, 31. Philadelphia: Fortress Press, 1957, pp. 127–8.

fellowship with God'.[23] All the same, Calvin was quick to stress that such psychological and spiritual affliction was at least as appalling as more tangible torment:

> ...unhappy consciences will find no rest from being troubled and tossed by a terrible whirlwind, from feeling that they are being torn asunder by a hostile Deity, pierced and lanced by deadly darts, quaking at God's lightning bolt, and being crushed by the weight of his hand – so that it would be more bearable to go down to any bottomless depths and chasms than to stand for a moment in these terrors.[24]

Fearsome analogies like this became commonplace among Calvin's followers, both in the writing and preaching of the Puritans, and then in the work of eighteenth century evangelists like Jonathan Edwards and George Whitefield. Edwards' famous sermon, 'Sinners in the Hands of an Angry God', may have unduly eclipsed his more profound theological work, but it reflects much evangelical preaching on hell during this period:

> O sinner! Consider the fearful danger you are in: it is a great furnace of wrath, a wide and bottomless pit, full of the fire of wrath, that you are held over in the hand of that God, whose wrath is provoked and incensed as much against you, as against many of the damned in hell. You hang by a slender thread, with the flames of divine wrath flashing about it, and ready every moment to singe it, and burn it asunder ...[25]

Although the Calvinist or Reformed tradition has supplied the bulk of apologetic material in support of eternal conscious punishment, it should not be forgotten that the Arminian John Wesley was also a firm proponent of it. Indeed, his sermon 'Of Hell' argued at some length that it is not only the fire which burns eternally, but also those whom it sears. Just as asbestos is heated but not consumed, so Wesley taught that sinners would suffer an eternal scalding of all that had given them wrongful

---

23. Calvin, *Institutes*, III:25:xii, p. 1007.
24. Calvin, *Institutes*, III:25:xii, p. 1008.
25. Preached July 8th, 1741 at Enfield. Reprinted in Edwards, Jonathan, *On Knowing Christ*, Edinburgh: Banner of Truth Trust, 1990.

pleasure on earth, without ever being annihilated. Besides, he reasoned, the fire of hell must have something continually to burn, or else it would go out.[26]

No doubt Wesley was reflecting the still-overwhelming consensus of his day, that hell was as it had been described by Tertullian, Lactantius, Augustine and the mainline Reformers: a sphere of just and relentless punishment which existed to satisfy the wrath of a God whom large numbers of men and women had spurned.

Over the course of the next two centuries, however, this consensus would gradually break down – due partly to the resurgence of universalism described in Chapter 2, but partly also to the emergence of conditional immortality as a serious challenge to the traditional view.

The Development of Conditionalism

Embryonic forms of conditionalist thinking can be inferred from the work of early church fathers like Ignatius, Justin Martyr, Theophilus of Antioch and the African rhetorician, Arnobius of Sicca.[27]

When writing of the Lord's Supper, Ignatius (c.35–110) describes eating communion bread as 'the medicine of immortality, the antidote that we should not die but live forever in Jesus Christ'.[28] The contrast here seems to be between eternal life and death, rather than between eternal life and eternal torment. Even so, it is unclear whether Ignatius

26. Cit. Fletcher, Caroline, 'Hell in the New Testament and Church History', Unpublished M.Phil, University of Sheffield, 1997, p. 229.

27. For more detailed accounts of relevant and potentially relevant patristic material see Froom, *Conditionalist Faith* (Vol. 1); Ellis, Earle, 'New Testament Teaching on Hell' in K.E. Brower & M.W. Elliott (eds.), *'The Reader Must Understand': Eschatology in the Bible and Theology*, Leicester: Apollos, 1997, pp. 199–205; Blanchard, John, *Whatever*, pp. 211–2.

28. Lightfoot, J.B., Holmes, M.W. & Harmer, J.R., *The Apostolic Fathers*, Grand Rapids: Baker Book House, 1998 (Originally London, 1885) 5,II,I,87.

himself would have taken the former distinction necessarily to exclude the latter, and in any case his immediate frame of reference seems to be Jesus' teaching in John 6, which bears only tangentially on the matter of hell. Ignatius' doctrine is simply not systematic enough on this issue for modern conditionalists to cite him in support of their case. Nonetheless, it is an intriguing and very early comment.

Rather more evidence of a 'proto-conditionalist' approach is available in the writings of Justin Martyr (c.100–165). In his *Apology*, Justin portrays an apocalyptic 'destruction of the whole cosmos, in order that evil angels, demons and men may no longer exist'.[29] Further, in his *Dialogue with Trypho*, he contrasts the immortality of 'those who appear worthy of God' with the 'perishable nature' of those who live without him. The latter, he adds, are duly 'punished' and must then 'die'.[30] It is also worth noting that this comment forms part of a discussion in which Justin identifies those who take the soul to be immortal as 'Platonists'. Justin's student, Tatian, later contended against such Platonists when arguing that the soul was, in fact, subject to death.[31]

Theophilus of Antioch (c.190) also appears to have seen eternity as a good gift of God to those who believe, rather than as the natural condition of all humanity:

> Man was neither mortal nor immortal by nature . . . but was able to receive both. If he [kept] . . . the command of God, he would receive immortality as a reward from Him and would become [like] God, but if he . . . [disobeyed] God, he would be responsible for his own death . . . Everyone who performs [God's commands] can be saved and, attaining to the resurrection, can inherit imperishability.[32]

---

29. *Apology*, 7:1.
30. 'Dialogue with Trypho', ed. & trans. Thomas B. Falls in *Saint Justin Martyr*, Washington DC: Catholic University of America Press, 1948 5:3ff.
31. 'Dialogue with Trypho', 5:1. Tatian, *Address to the Greeks (Oratio ad Graecos)*, Trans. Molly Whittaker, Oxford: Clarendon Press, 1982, 13:1.
32. Theophilus of Antioch, *Ad Autolycum*, ed. & trans. R.M. Grant, Oxford: Oxford University Press, 1970, pp. 69ff.

While these early theologians focused more generally on the fate of the soul in God's purposes, Arnobius (died c. 330) provides the first explicit defence of the annihilation of ungodly souls in hell. It must be noted that Arnobius is among the least biblically-grounded of the early church fathers. Even so, he drew a significant distinction between the eternity of hellfire itself as a *means* of judgment, and the finite existence of those who are plunged into that fire as *objects* of judgment – objects who are eventually consumed by the flames and so 'destroyed forever':

> They are cast in, and being annihilated, pass away vainly in everlasting destruction . . . this is man's real death, which leaves nothing behind. For that which is seen by the eyes is [only] a separation of soul from body, not the last end – annihilation: this, I say, is man's real death, when souls which know not God shall be consumed in long-protracted torment with raging fire . . . [33]

It is important to note here that Arnobius manages to combine the familiar notion of drawn-out anguish with the idea of final destruction. The annihilation he proposes is not immediate upon death, and therefore need not bypass final resurrection and judgment. [34] In this respect, it differs from the annihilationist models proposed by more recent Christian sects, including the Socinians and the Christadelphians (see Chapter 4). [35] Despite this, the annihilationist approach was deemed heretical by the Second Council of Constantinople in 553 and again by the Lateran Council in 1513, although neither named Arnobius explicitly, and may not have known of his particular work on the issue.

---

33. Arnobius, *The Seven Books of Arnobius Adversus Gentes*, Ante-Nicene Christian Library, vol. 19; Edinburgh: T&T Clark, 1871, 79–81, 2:14.

34. Cf. The inference drawn by Peterson, *Hell on Trial*, p. 104.

35. On Socinian eschatology see Wilbur, E.M., *A History of Unitarianism: Socinianism and Its Antecedents*, Cambridge: Cambridge University Press, 1952. On Christadelphian understanding see Davies, Eryl, *Truth Under Attack: Cults and Contemporary Religions*, Darlington: Evangelical Press, pp. 105–111.

Although it reappeared in the writings of the Cornish Socinian John Biddle,[36] and in the work of the eighteenth century philosopher William Whiston,[37] this view only began to regain credibility within the mainline churches during the Victorian age. Indeed, as Geoffrey Rowell has shown, the mid-nineteenth century period – the period in which the Evangelical Alliance was formed – was marked by a remarkable rise of interest, among evangelicals as well as others, in alternative views on hell and the afterlife.[38]

Until the mid-1800s the main challenge to the traditionalist doctrine of eternal conscious punishment had come from universalism. Now, however, a growing number of theologians began to seek a 'middle way'. While rejecting definitions of restitution as a *remission* of judgment for all, they nonetheless recast it as a *positive consequence* of judgment for the redeemed – something which must follow on from God's condemnation and destruction of wicked people and things at the end of the age. One major factor in all of this was the growth of Unitarianism.

Unitarianism had been formalised into a denominational structure by Theophilus Lindsey in 1773, but had influenced other Protestant traditions before then, and continued to do so afterwards. In addition to their rejection of the trinity, the early Unitarians tended to teach the annihilation of the wicked, even if most of their successors would go on to embrace systematic universalism.[39]

Unitarianism was reaching its peak at the time of the foundation of the Evangelical Alliance in 1846 – not least in North America. Indeed, it was partly in reaction to the Unitarian-sponsored spread of annihilationist views that the American delegation at the inaugural conference of the 'World's Evangelical Alliance' in 1846 pressed for the inclusion

---

36. Fletcher, Caroline, 'Hell in the New Testament and Church History'. Unpublished M.Phil, University of Sheffield, 1997, p. 175–6.

37. For an account see Peterson, *Hell on Trial*, pp. 120–2.

38. Rowell, *Hell and the Victorians*.

39. For more detail see Rowell, *Hell and the Victorians*; Fletcher, 'Hell', pp. 233–7.

of a clause affirming 'the eternal punishment of the wicked' in the new body's Basis of Faith. The preliminary draft drawn up by the British divisions of the Alliance the year before had, in fact, omitted to deal with eschatology from *any* perspective, so this was a significant clarification.[40] Even so, once incorporated into the official text of the Basis, it would soon prove contentious.

Partly in response to the final wording of the 1846 Basis, the former Unitarian-turned-Anglican F.D. Maurice published a book of *Theological Essays* in which he argued that the phrase usually translated 'eternal punishment' in Matthew 25:46 referred to the quality of God's retribution, rather than its duration. In particular, he contended, it should be understood to denote 'the punishment of being without the knowledge of God', rather than a physical and everlasting torment in hell-fire.[41] Maurice was dismissed from his Chair at King's College, London for expressing these views. Even so, they were growing ever more popular – a fact evident not only in the backing given to them by the liberal authors of the landmark volume *Essays and Reviews* (1860), but also in events which would soon shake EA to its foundations.

In 1868, the honorary secretary of the Alliance's British Organisation, T.R. Birks, was censured for publishing a book called *The Victory of Divine Goodness*. Birks advocated a qualified restitutionism in which 'the lost' had the potential to develop in the afterlife to a point where they could eventually share some of the joy of God's re-made cosmos, if not its full blessings. He held that this was consistent with the Alliance's theology, and in a way, it was. His scheme *did* maintain unbelievers in an eternal realm rather than annihilating them, and this eternal realm *was* divided off from heaven. It was, however, palliative (if not exactly remedial), and this hardly reflected the intent of those Americans who had first inserted the clause on

40. Kessler, *Evangelical Alliance*, p. 34.
41. Maurice, F.D., *Theological Essays (2nd. Edn.)*, London: James Clarke & Co, Ltd., 1853, p. 450.

hell into the Basis. After much wrangling over whether the British Organisation could legitimately expel an original member of the World's Evangelical Alliance, Birks tendered his resignation. As if this were not painful enough, when a significant minority of Council members failed to secure a formal condemnation of Birks's views, 15 of them resigned in protest at the Council's moderate stance. This in turn led to a crippling dispute about the authority of the Alliance, and its right to examine the private judgment of individuals who had signed its statement of faith.[42] As a result, no annual conferences were held in 1870 or 1872, and for the years 1871–1874 annual reports were either withheld or significantly truncated.[43]

In the 1870s and 1880s, prominent figures like Edward White and Henry Constable further popularised conditionalist thought, and gained a degree of acceptance for it within Anglican and larger Free Church constituencies – an acceptance which grew gradually through the ensuing decades.[44] Furthermore, even if evangelicals remained overwhelmingly opposed to conditionalism, the first half of the twentieth century saw a limited number moving publicly to support it. The CMS missionary Harold Guillebaud was one notable example; the prominent Inter-Varsity Fellowship leader and staunch evangelical apologist Basil F.C. Atkinson was another.[45] Even then, however, it is significant that both Guillebaud's *The Righteous Judge* (1941) and Atkinson's *Life and Immortality* (1964) were published privately and circulated to a very small readership. Against this background, the revision of the Evangelical Alliance's Basis of Faith in 1967–70 takes on particular significance.

Among several other changes, the EA dropped direct reference to 'eternal punishment' from the Basis in 1970. Instead, it left members to infer its position on hell from two revised

---

42. For further detail on this see Kessler, *Evangelical Alliance*, pp. 67–9.

43. Kessler, *Evangelical Alliance*, p. 69.

44. Froom, *Conditionalist Faith (Vol 2)*.

45. For an account and references see Fudge, *Fire*, p. 9.

clauses on human sin. The first of these (Clause 3) affirms 'the universal sinfulness and guilt of fallen man' as a just cause of 'God's *wrath and condemnation*' (our emphasis). The other (Clause 4) declares Christ's substitutionary sacrifice on the cross to be the only basis of redemption from the '*eternal consequences*' of sin. The emphasis on eternity here clearly echoes traditionalist language. Even so, it does not necessarily exclude conditionalists, who often argue that the *instrument* of punishment may itself be everlasting, but that the *effect* of God's penalty for any specific individual is terminal.[46] This interpretation is given further credence by the fact that the person who has done most in recent times to raise the profile of conditionalism in the UK – the Anglican evangelical leader John Stott – was active in the 1967–70 redrafting of the Basis.[47]

In 1988, Stott published a 'Liberal–Evangelical Dialogue' with his fellow-Anglican David L. Edwards. This involved a discussion of hell, in which Stott leaned towards conditionalism while finally declaring himself to be 'tentative' about whether it should replace the traditional view.[48] Stott's arguments echoed those which had been put forward by Guillebaud and Atkinson, but especially resonated with the stance which had been taken 14 years previously by another Anglican evangelical, John Wenham. In his 1974 study *The Goodness of God*, Wenham had offered careful arguments which gained a respectful hearing and prompted some lively responses.[49] Not least, he inspired the American scholar Edward William Fudge to produce a full-length survey of the biblical material which rapidly became the standard

---

46. For an account of this view, with supporting references, see Fudge, *Fire*, pp. 11–20.
47. Stott at the time convened the Alliance's Theological Study Group, to which the amendment process was referred. Minutes of the Executive Council, 67/11–12 (19.1.67); 67/51 (27.7.67).
48. Stott, *Essentials*, pp. 320.
49. Wenham, John, *The Goodness of God*, Leicester: IVP, 1974. Later reprinted as *The Enigma of Evil*, 1985.

reference-work on evangelical conditionalism.[50] Subsequently, at a major conference on hell in 1992, Wenham expounded his position in a paper entitled 'The Case for Conditional Immortality'.[51] The book based on this conference represents just one in a cascade of works on hell produced by evangelicals in the period since Stott made his views known.[52]

In the next chapter, we shall draw on this more recent literature to chart a course through what is becoming an increasingly complex debate. In doing so, we shall need to expand and refine the categories with which we have been working. Our basic distinction between eternal conscious punishment and conditionalism may have sufficed thus far, but it does not reflect all the nuances with which we must deal.

---

50. Fudge, *Fire*, pp. 9–10.

51. In Cameron, Nigel M. de S (ed.), *Universalism and the Doctrine of Hell*, Carlisle: Paternoster, 1992, pp. 161–90. For Wenham's personal reflections on this debate, and on its antecedents, see *Facing Hell: An Autobiography 1913–1996*, Carlisle: Paternoster, 1998, pp. 229–257.

52. For a useful summary of the debate and relevant references, see Gray, 'Destroyed for Ever'.

5

The Doctrine of Hell Among Evangelicals
Today: I. Defining the Main Positions

We have already stated that this report has been compiled in
response to growing disagreement among contemporary
evangelicals on the nature of hell. Against such a background it
is particularly important that the different positions taken in
the debate are fairly and accurately represented. To do this, we
shall need to sharpen our definitions before moving on to look
more closely at the relevant biblical and theological issues.

So far we have suggested that, apart from a small number
who either advocate or tend towards universalism, Christians
in the evangelical community have taken one of two main
positions on the nature of hell. Traditionalists hold that the
unredeemed will suffer eternal conscious punishment,
whereas conditionalists believe that they will ultimately be
destroyed. Beyond this dichotomy, however, further variations
must be recognised. Perhaps eternal conscious punishment is
only psychological and spiritual, rather than physical. Perhaps
it is preferable to speak more generally of separation from God,
rather than to spell out the detail of punishment in hell. If the
damned are ultimately destroyed, will they suffer any punishment before this destruction, or will it coincide with death, or
with final judgment? In the same scenario, will God himself
actively destroy the impenitent by depriving them of their

'immortal soul', or will the mortality they have inherited from Adam cause them to perish automatically? In either case, will their extinction be gradual or relatively swift?

Faced with complications like these, a number of more subtle models have been proposed. For example, David Powys lists 12, or even possibly 15, different positions on the afterlife and hell, of which at least seven are associated with evangelicals.[1] The details of Powys' classification depend on how each theologian responds to the key criteria of the duration, the finality, the quality and the purpose of hell. For our context, it will be sufficient to define five distinct positions within the broader categories of traditionalism and conditionalism. In so doing we aim to encompass a wide variety of views in a simplified manner, whilst clearly marking the most important distinctions. The five positions are as follows:

1. Eternal Conscious Physical & Spiritual Torment

2. Eternal Conscious Spiritual Torment

3. Eternal Separation from God

4. Conditional Immortality

5. Annihilationism

First, we shall briefly summarise these five positions and identify their key proponents in the recent debate about hell. Having done this, we shall examine in detail the main exegetical and theological concerns to which these positions are related.

1. Eternal Conscious Physical and Spiritual Torment

This view holds that occupants of hell will knowingly endure bodily and spiritual punishment. Its advocates stress that, however harsh it may seem, the plain teaching of Scripture, not least of Jesus himself, points to such a fate. In this perspective the

---

1. Powys, 'Hell and Universalism', pp. 137–8.

undying worm and endless fire of Isaiah 66:24 and Mark 9:48 plainly denote conscious eternal suffering. Likewise Matthew 25:46, where Jesus parallels 'eternal punishment' for the wicked with 'eternal life' for the righteous. Furthermore, the ever-rising smoke and unending restlessness of those who worship the beast and his image in Revelation 14:11 are read as clear references to everlasting physical and mental torment. Supporters of this view often cite Revelation 20:10, with its vivid portrait of those whose names are omitted from the book of life being 'thrown into the lake of fire' and 'tormented day and night for ever and ever'. For these traditionalists, proper biblical theology will emphasise a God who justly demands that sin should be punished. Unredeemed sin against an infinitely good God is thus defined as infinite in consequence – that is, deserving of endless retribution.

As we have made clear, this view is the one most widely attested in church history. Moreover, despite being qualified or abandoned by many in the wider church today, all available evidence suggests that it remains the dominant understanding of hell among evangelical Christians.[2] Prominent advocates for it include Robert Morey, John Gerstner, James Packer, Ajith Fernando, David Pawson, John Blanchard, Robert Peterson and Donald Carson.[3]

---

2. We have already referred in Chapter 1 to the 1998 Evangelical Alliance survey which showed 79.6% of member churches affirming eternal punishment as against 14.2% who related hell to the annihilation of the unsaved. A helpful digest of various surveys of North American evangelicals on this matter is presented by James Davison Hunter in his book *Evangelicalism: The Coming Generation* (Chicago: University of Chicago Press, 1987), pp. 34–40. This shows consistent and strong majorities siding with the traditional view of hell as eternal torment, although Hunter does detect some softening and qualifying of this stance in the more recent studies with which he deals. Similarly, while George Marsden found 86% of students at Fuller Theological Seminary affirming 'eternal torment for those who do not believe in Jesus Christ' in 1982, his questioning of alumni from previous periods showed up to one-fifth moving away from this view at some point after they had graduated (*Reforming Fundamentalism*, Grand Rapids: Eerdmans, 1987, p. 304).

3. Morey, R.A., *Death and the Afterlife*, Minneapolis: Bethany, 1984; Gerstner, John, *Repent or Perish*, Ligonier, PA.: Soli Deo Gloria, 1990; Packer, J.I. *The Problem of*

2. Eternal Conscious Spiritual Torment

In this perspective, those condemned to hell will be subjected to genuine psychological and spiritual torment, but will not endure *physical* suffering. Proponents of this view argue that images used to convey the terror of hell in Scripture need not be read as denoting material pain. They accept that the familiar biblical references to worms, fire and gnashing teeth portray genuine anguish and remorse, but argue that they are not to be read literally. Rather, advocates of this position often point out that it may in fact be *worse* to suffer spiritually – to be estranged from God for ever – than to endure endless physical punishment. Contemporary evangelical proponents of this view include Anthony Hoekema, Murray Harris and Peter Toon.[4]

3. Eternal Separation from God

A third, less specific stance is that those in hell will be eternally separated from God. Rather than become preoccupied with the precise workings of hell, advocates of this stance focus on the *relational* consequences of faith and unbelief. They stress that humanity was created for communion with God and view this as being the essence of salvation and the gospel. Those who find themselves in hell are therefore those who lack such communion. By the same token, the biblical images of fire, destruction and punishment are taken to define a worse reality – the fact that human beings will be estranged from the love of God. 'Separationists' characteristically contend that we are not

3. (*continued*) *Eternal Punishment*. Disley: Orthos, 1990; Fernando, Ajith, *Crucial Questions About Hell*, Eastbourne: Kingsway, 1991; Pawson, *Road to Hell*; Blanchard, John, *Whatever*; Peterson, *Hell on Trial*; Carson, D.A., *The Gagging of God: Christianity Confronts Pluralism*, Leicester: Apollos, 1996, pp. 515–36.
4. Hoekema, Anthony A., *The Bible and the Future*, Exeter: Paternoster, 1979, pp. 265–73; Harris, M.J., *Raised Immortal*, London: Marshall, Morgan and Scott, 1983; Toon, Peter, *Longing for the Heavenly Realm: The Missing Element in Modern Western Spirituality*, London: Hodder & Stoughton, 1986.

called to speculate at length as to what exactly this means. Even so, one of the most widely read books on hell published in the twentieth century, C.S. Lewis' *The Great Divorce*, presents a vivid allegory of salvation and damnation based largely on this concept.[5] Indeed, Lewis does much to remind traditionalists and conditionalists alike that hell must be viewed in *relational* as well as purely *mechanical* terms – that is, as 'privation' from the love of God rather than merely as endless torture or extinction.[6]

Whether they acknowledge a debt to Lewis or not, many of the evangelicals who emphasise this aspect of hell do not do so to the exclusion of eternal conscious punishment, but see it as a necessary check on undue relish at the torments of the lost, and on the 'folk' tradition of hell encouraged by the lurid paintings of Pieter Breughel, Hieronymus Bosch and others. Among these are Kendall Harmon, Alec Motyer and Peter Head.[7] Then again, Stephen Travis, who leans towards conditionalism, also casts hell in largely separationist terms.[8]

4. Conditional Immortality

In this report we have followed the now common practice of using the term 'conditionalism' to describe the view that hell means final destruction rather than eternal conscious punishment. Strictly speaking, however, conditionalism defines a particular view on the destiny of the soul – namely, that it is not *inherently* immortal, but *acquires* immortality as a condition of justification by grace through faith. Hence the more

5. Lewis, C.S., *The Great Divorce*, Glasgow: Fontana, 1972 [1946]. **Great Divorce**.
6. A point made by Harmon, Kendall, 'The Case Against Conditionalism', in Cameron, Nigel M. de S. (ed.), *Universalism and the Doctrine of Hell*, Carlisle: Paternoster, 1992, pp. 216–224.
7. Harmon, 'Case Against Conditionalism', pp. 216–224; Motyer, Alec, *After Death*, Fearn: Christian Focus, 1996; Head, 'Duration'.
8. Travis, Stephen, *Christ and the Judgment of God: Divine Retribution in the New Testament*, Basingstoke: Marshall, Morgan and Scott, 1986.

technical description 'conditional immortality', where 'immortality' means an inability to perish. Far from being intrinsic to all human beings, eternal existence is taken to be dependent on salvation. Conditionalists often stress that this heavenly life will be eternal in both *quantitative* and *qualitative* terms, the former referring to the *duration*, and the latter to the *type* of existence. By contrast, they believe that the unrighteous will cease to exist, thereby bearing out their mortality apart from Christ. Indeed, a key text for conditionalists is Romans 6:23: 'The wages of sin is death, but the gift of God is eternal life.' The marginal form of conditionalism propounded by sectarian groups like the Socinians and Christadelphians equates 'death' here with the end of earthly life. Evangelical conditionalists, however, typically relate it to the extinction of the impenitent either straight after they have been resurrected and judged, or after a time of punishment in hell following judgment.[9]

Conditionalists argue that most people equate the biblical view of hell with eternal conscious punishment because this has become deeply ingrained within the Christian tradition. Specifically, they maintain that Greek philosophy unduly affected early church teaching on this matter. From their perspective it was Hellenistic assumptions about the immortality of the soul, rather than scriptural revelation itself, which accounted for the doctrine. Indeed, conditionalists routinely call attention to the imagery of destruction, perishing and extinction which pervades New Testament eschatology, and seek to interpret the language of divine retribution and human suffering in this context, rather than *vice versa*.

We have already identified John Wenham and Edward Fudge as leading evangelical apologists for conditionalism.

---

9. On this basis, Kendall Harmon and Norman T. Burns describe the evangelical version of conditionalism as *mortalist eventual extinctionism*. Burns, Norman T., *Christian Mortalism from Tyndale to Milton*, Cambridge, Mass.: Harvard University Press, 1972. Harmon, 'Case against Conditionalism', pp. 196–7. This is a distinction which John Stott appears not to have acknowledged: *Essentials*, p. 316.

Others include Michael Green, Clark Pinnock, Robert Brow, Nigel Wright and Earle Ellis.[10]

5. Annihilationism

We have seen that annihilation of the wicked is the logical *consequence* of conditional immortality. Theoretically, however, it is worth pointing out that it need not depend on conditionalist *assumptions*: it does not absolutely *require* the 'original mortality' of humankind. Indeed, it would be possible to advocate it while maintaining a 'classical' belief in the immortality of the soul if one asserted that God actively *deprives* the unrighteous of this immortality at some point after final judgment, with the result that they then perish. Thus, rather than defining immortality as something *conferred* by God (as in conditionalism), this view would take it to be something which might be *confiscated* by God. In practice, however, this remains little more than a formal distinction: even Kendall Harmon, who makes it, acknowledges that it is 'artificial' in relation to theologies of hell as they have actually been produced.[11] The reality is that those evangelicals who have propounded the annihilation of the lost in contemporary debate about hell have done so from a conditionalist foundation. Hence our use of the term 'conditionalism' to cover belief in both conditional immortality *and* eventual extinction of the unredeemed.

---

10. Wenham, John, 'The Case for Conditional Immortality', in Cameron, Nigel M. de S. (ed.) *Universalism and the Doctrine of Hell*, Carlisle: Paternoster, 1992, pp. 161–91; also *Facing Hell*; Fudge, *Fire*; Green, Michael, *Evangelism Through the Local Church*, London: Hodder & Stoughton, 1990, pp. 69f.; Pinnock, Clark H. & Brow, Robert C., *Unbounded Love: A Good News Theology for the 21st Century*, Carlisle: Paternoster, 1994, pp. 87–95; Ellis, Earle, 'New Testament Teaching on Hell', in Brower, K.E. and Elliott, M.W. (eds.), '*The Reader Must Understand': Eschatology in Bible and Theology*, Leicester: Apollos, 1997; Wright, Nigel, *The Radical Evangelical: Seeking a Place to Stand*, London: SPCK, 1996, pp. 87–102.

11. A position dubbed *immortalist extinctionism* by Harmon: 'Case against Conditionalism' pp. 197.

Some further points need to be made here. Annihilation as conceived by evangelical conditionalists should obviously be distinguished from the humanist belief that there is no life *of any kind* after death, and that *all* persons go into oblivion once they have breathed their last. As we have seen, evangelical writers who affirm the final destruction of the unrighteous accept that it will occur only after resurrection and final judgment, and usually also envisage a period of divine punishment before extinction. In this sense, it would be misleading to pronounce them guilty by association with 'sects' and 'cults'. Christadelphians may teach immediate destruction at death for all non-elect persons, and Jehovah's Witnesses may reserve final resurrection for the righteous alone, but these are not the views of any self-professed evangelical conditionalist we have read.[12] Admittedly, somewhat closer parallels can be drawn with Seventh Day Adventism, which takes annihilation to be the 'end-point' of divine punishment, rather than its entire content.[13] Even here, however, the mere fact of a resemblance can be taken to imply neither a causal connection on this particular point, nor a more general infiltration of Adventist theology into evangelical conditionalism.

---

12. As we mentioned in the Introduction, John Stott could be read as diverging slightly from this norm. This is to say, he seems to favour annihilation without specifying a clearly conditionalist motive for doing so. This may, however, simply be due to his implication that 'conditionalists' believe *ipso facto* in immediate rather than eventual extinction, *Essentials*, p. 316. On the Christadelphian view see Davies, *Truth Under Attack*, p. 110; on Jehovah's Witness understanding of hell see Clarke, Eric & Sanderson, Ruth, *Aid to Watchtower Understanding*, Faversham: Christian Information Outreach, n.d., p. 4; Tucker, Ruth: *Strange Gospels*, London: Marshall Pickering, 1989, p. 141; Davies, *Truth Under Attack*, p. 141, 143. Specifically, the Jehovah's Witness doctrine is that an 'anointed class' of 144,000 will rule over the earth once Jesus has returned to Jerusalem, and that during this period there will be a 'resurrection of judgment' in which the unrighteous will be annihilated, but in which some others who have responded to the truth after Christ's return will be rewarded with eternal life. The concept of hell as a place of eternal punishment is dismissed as a pagan idea and a cruel deception of Satan.
13. For a helpful categorisation of these very different forms of annihilationism see Harmon, 'Case against Conditionalism', pp. 196–7.

We have seen that conditionalism addresses a key issue in theological anthropology – namely, whether or not the soul is immortal. However, while they might diverge on this question, evangelicals would agree with the more basic proposition that God alone has the power to give and take away life. On this basis in fact, some traditionalists have conceded that, although innate immortality exists due to God's sovereign grace in creation, the same sovereign God could *in principle* withdraw it from sinners and thus annihilate them. In the end, of course, these traditionalists maintain that God has *actually* chosen to order things in such a way as to rule out annihilation as a corollary of hell. Still, the point is important with respect to the doctrine of God and its relation to the doctrine of man.[14]

★   ★   ★

The positions outlined above clearly reflect different approaches to the biblical text. Indeed, one of the key issues in the current debate about hell is that of hermeneutics, or the interpretation of Scripture. There is not room here to provide an exhaustive account of every hermeneutical point made in the burgeoning evangelical literature on hell. In the next two chapters we shall, however, seek to present the main points of exegetical and theological concern.

---

14. For detailed exposition on these points see Harmon, 'Case against Conditionalism', pp. 198–9

6

The Doctrine of Hell Among Evangelicals Today: II. Key Exegetical Issues

Destruction and Perishing

Much of the evangelical debate about hell turns on biblical semantics. As we have seen, conditionalists maintain that scriptural language points towards annihilation rather than eternal conscious punishment. In particular, they argue that in the New Testament *apollymi* (usually translated 'destroy') implies the eventual termination of existence rather than the perpetuation of torment. John Stott exemplifies this approach when he notes that, just as Herod's move to 'destroy' the infant Jesus at Matthew 2:13 conveys intent to end a life, so when Jesus later warns against the one who 'can destroy both soul and body in hell', there is a contrast with Greek philosophical concept of the eternal soul, with hell pictured instead as a realm of obliteration (Matt. 10:28).[1] Traditionalists reply that other references to destruction, whether featuring *apollymi* or synonyms such as *olethros,* can connote a process of ongoing 'lostness' or eternal 'perishing' in which the object itself remains in existence (Matt. 10:6; Luke 15:4; 6, 8, 9, 24, 32;

---

1. *Essentials,* p. 315. For parallels see also Pinnock & Brow, *Unbounded Love,* pp. 91–2; Fudge, *Fire* pp. 105–9; Hughes, P.E. *The True Image,* Leicester: IVP, 1989, pp. 398–407.

Thess. 1:9; 2 Pet. 2:3).[2] This, however, does not persuade John
Stott. As far as he is concerned, 'it would seem strange . . . if
people who are said to suffer destruction are in fact not
destroyed; and . . . it is difficult to imagine a perpetually incon-
clusive process of perishing'.[3]

This dispute about the general terminology of destruction is
sharpened in exegetical disagreements over specific biblical
images of hell.

The Fire and the Worm

A second point of disagreement concerns the biblical imagery of fire. Conditionalists argue from the common-sense
premise that the main purpose of fire is not to inflict sensory
pain, but to destroy. Although biblical fire has traditionally
been associated with eternal conscious punishment, they hold
that extinction would more naturally result from it.[4] Traditionalist objections to this line of reasoning are numerous.
Not least, they oppose it by underlining that the worm and
fire in the key text Mark 9:48 are respectively *undying* and
unquenchable. Indeed, this forms the centrepiece of Donald
Carson's robust defence of eternal punishment, and features
prominently in the apologetic work of Blanchard, Hoekema
and Head on the same issue.[5] Conditionalists, however,
maintain that this imagery does not *in and of itself* necessitate
the endless torture of each individual sinner. Stott, for
example, argues that Jesus here tellingly avoids any clear
inference of everlasting pain from his source text in Isaiah
66:24 – even if the intertestamental book of Judith had made

---

2. See Hoekema, *Future*, pp. 269–70; Fernando, *Crucial Questions*, pp. 40–1.
3. Stott, *Essentials*, p. 316.
4. Wenham, 'Conditional Immortality', p. 171; Travis, *Second Coming of Jesus*,
p. 198; Stott, *Essentials*, p. 316; Fudge, *Fire*, pp. 66–8; Wright, *Radical Evangelical*;
Pinnock & Brow, *Unbounded Love*, p. 91.
5. E.g. Carson, *Gagging of God*, pp. 524ff.; Blanchard, *Whatever*, pp. 136–45; Head,
'Duration'; Hoekema, *Future*, p. 268.

such associations (Jud. 16:17).[6] Conversely, Fernando takes the Judith text to confirm that the natural interpretation of fire in the Jewish mind related to pain rather than destruction.[7] Stott, however, is persuaded that, although both the worm and the fire *themselves* appear to be everlasting, the *effect* they have on any individual sinner may yet be terminal.[8] Against this view, Blanchard emphasises the use of 'their' worm, suggesting that the possessive indicates the sinner's individual conscience, which 'gnaws away' at him into all eternity.[9] From the conditionalist side, Fudge and Nigel Wright counter that this need not be so, since the root imagery from Isaiah refers to a worm which devours what is *already dead*.[10]

Eternal Punishment and 'The Age to Come'

Probably the most commonly cited text in defence of the traditional position is Matthew 25:46. Here, Jesus appears to draw a straight parallel between 'eternal life' and 'eternal punishment', applying the same adjective (*aiōnios*) to both states. Since it is clear that Jesus offers genuinely everlasting, unending life to those who follow him, surely, the logic goes, he must be warning of a retribution which will be correspondingly everlasting and unending for those who refuse him.[11] The standard conditionalist reply to such exegesis suggests that our preconceptions force us to read the text in this manner, whereas the passage never in fact defines the precise nature of

6. *Essentials*, p. 317. A similar approach is adopted by Wenham, 'Conditional Immortality', p. 178, and Fudge, *Fire*, pp. 62–5.

7. Fernando, *Crucial Questions*, p. 79.

8. *Essentials*, p. 317. For examples of the same argument see Wright, *Radical Evangelical*, p. 93; Ellis, 'New Testament Teaching', pp. 212–4.

9. Blanchard, *Whatever* p. 148 & p. 230

10. Fudge, *Fire*, p. 185; Wright, *Radical Evangelical*, pp. 92–3.

11. For examples of this argument see Carson, *Gagging of God*, pp. 523, 528–9; Gerstner, *Repent or Perish*, pp. 92–9, 150–8; Packer, *Eternal Punishment*, p. 3.

the 'eternal' states to which it refers. Certainly, conditionalists accept that it equates redeemed 'life' as everlasting with divine 'punishment' as everlasting, but they characteristically point out that this punishment could be the punishment of destruction – a punishment which is no less real than ongoing torture, but which would be eternal in overall *effect* rather than in the personal consciousness of every condemned sinner.[12] From this point of view, Stephen Travis echoes the often-asserted conditionalist point that a better translation of Matthew 25:46 would be less precisely chronological – that is, 'the punishment of the age to come' and 'the life of the age to come'. For Travis, Powys and other conditionalists, this rendering conveys the fact that *aiōnios* should be understood in the wider context of biblical eschatology, as an adjective of *quality* rather than *quantity* – one that defines a new order of being which cannot finally be measured in terms of time.[13] The traditionalist riposte to all this, however, has been to wonder whether the word 'eternal' could really change its meaning so markedly from one phrase to the other.[14] Traditionalists have also routinely drawn parallels with Revelation 14:11 and 20:10, where the same word features in the more emphatic time adverbs *aiōnas aiōnon* and *aiōnas ton aiōnon*, meaning 'for ever and ever' or 'to the ages of ages' (see below). Furthermore, Carson has argued that the dominant understanding of such vocabulary in first century Palestinian Judaism would have related it to eternal conscious punishment rather than to eventual extinction.[15]

12. See Fudge, *Fire*, pp. 119–25; Powys, *Hard Look*, pp. 291–3; Ellis, 'New Testament Teaching', pp. 214–6.
13. Travis, *Second Coming*, p. 199. For parallels see Ellis, 'New Testament Teaching', pp. 214–6; Powys, *Hard Look*, p. 292; Wright, *Radical Evangelical*, p. 93.
14. Eg. Carson, *Gagging of God*, pp. 528–9; Gerstner, *Repent or Perish*, pp. 92–9; Peterson, *Hell on Trial*, pp. 195–8.
15. Carson, *Gagging of God*, p. 529. For a representative conditionalist treatment of the contemporary uses of *aionios* see Fudge, *Fire*, pp. 11–20.

The Unbridgeable Gulf

Another New Testament passage often promoted in defence of eternal conscious punishment is Jesus' account of the rich man and Lazarus (Luke 16:19–31).[16] The rich man is described here as enduring 'torment', having been consigned to Hades. He is fully aware of his suffering, which appears to be both psychological *and* physical (v. 24). Even so, conditionalists have argued that there is no indication that his suffering will last forever.[17] In fact beyond this particular debate about the duration of punishment, biblical scholars diverge widely on how exactly this text should be interpreted. Its status in relation to the parables of Jesus is disputed, as is its relevance to the issue of whether there is an intermediate state between death and final resurrection. Furthermore, many scholars have doubted the legitimacy of inferring definitive dogmatic conclusions about the afterlife from so clearly generic, symbolic and metaphorical a narrative.[18] From a literary critical perspective, most now recognise that it is based on a well-established Near Eastern folk tale, of which several versions had been produced in Jewish literature at the time, and in which the central concerns were avarice, stewardship and pride rather than the mechanics of heaven and hell.[19] Bearing all this in mind, it is advisable to focus on the more transparent aspects of the text, without indulging in undue speculation.

The two key points here are the reversed fortunes of the rich man and Lazarus, and the decisive nature of their eternal fate.

16. For examples of this text's use by traditionalists see North, Brownlow, *The Rich Man and Lazarus: An Exposition of Luke 16:19–31*, Edinburgh: The Banner of Truth Trust, 1979 [1859]; Pawson, *Road to Hell*, pp. 121–9; Peterson, *Hell on Trial*, pp. 65–68; Dixon, Larry, *The Other Side of the Good News*, Wheaton, Ill.: Bridgepoint, 1992, pp. 130–44.

17. Stott, *Essentials*, pp. 317–8; Fudge, *Fire*, p. 126 n.103.

18. For a summary of the critical debate see Marshall, I. Howard, *The Gospel of Luke*, Exeter: Paternoster, 1978, pp. 632–39; Powys, *Hard Look*, pp. 218–45.

19. See Creed, H.M. *St. Luke*, London: Macmillan, 1930; Marshall, I. Howard, *The Gospel of Luke*, Exeter: Paternoster, 1978, pp. 632–4; Travis, *Second Coming*, p. 197; Stott, *Essentials*, p. 316f.

Traditionalists hold that Jesus' reference to Lazarus' 'finger' and the rich man's burning 'tongue' in v. 24 must signify the final state of things, since all will by then have been re-united with their physical bodies, raised to judgment and sent for eternity to heaven or hell.[20] Conditionalists, however, point out that this reading is inconsistent with the continued existence of the rich man's house and five brothers on earth (v. 27), and with the fact that the Hades in which he suffers will eventually come to an end as it is 'cast into the lake of fire' at the close of the age (Rev. 20:14).[21]

Sulphur, Smoke and the 'Second Death'

Another key point of dispute among evangelicals is the meaning of Revelation 14:10. Here apostates who worship the beast and his image are to be 'tormented with burning sulphur in the presence of the holy angels and of the Lamb'. Furthermore, 'the smoke of their torment rises for ever and ever. There is no rest day and night for those who worship the beast and his image, or for anyone who receives the mark of his name'. Traditional apologists regularly contend that the plain sense of this text clinches the argument for eternal conscious punishment.[22] Indeed, John Wenham concedes that this is 'the most difficult passage that the conditionalist has to deal with', admitting that 'on the face of it, having no rest day or night with smoke of torment going up for ever and ever, sounds like everlasting torment'.[23] Nevertheless, he follows Fudge and Stott in drawing a parallel with God's destruction of Sodom in Genesis 19, Edom in Isaiah 34 and Gog in Ezekiel 38, all of which are reduced to wastes of burning sulphur, but which themselves cease to exist as cities once they have been razed to the ground.

---

20. Pawson, *Road to Hell*, pp. 128–9; Blanchard, *Whatever*, pp. 81, 154.
21. Fudge, *Fire*, p. 129; Wenham, 'Conditional Immortality', pp. 179–80.
22. Hoekema, *Future*, p. 272; Head, 'Duration', pp. 226–7; Carson, *Gagging of God*, pp. 526–7; Blanchard, *Whatever*, pp. 229–30.
23. Wenham, 'Conditional Immortality', p. 179.

In other words, conditionalists argue that the main purpose of the fire is to consume what it burns, and the rising smoke which results is merely a trace of the destruction which that fire has wrought.[24] Earle Ellis makes the same point with regard to Jude 7, which, he says, does not suggest that Sodom *itself* is ever-burning, 'but that the burning lasts for ever'.[25] Stott deduces from all this that the 'torment' endured by the unrighteous here must relate to their 'moment of judgment' and not to their 'eternal state'. Wenham sees support for such a reading in Luke 12:9, where those who disown Christ on earth will themselves be disowned 'before the angels of God'.[26]

Against such exegesis, traditionalists like Blanchard, Harmon and Carson stress, as with Isaiah 66:24 and Mark 9:48 ('*their* worm'), that we cannot so easily pass over the link between the possessive pronoun and the depiction of eternal suffering. These scholars argue that if the torment portrayed in John's vision as '*their* torment' is torment which *belongs personally* to those who bear the mark of the beast, and if that torment is 'for ever and ever', then we must surely infer eternal conscious punishment from the text. Carson adds that the Greek phrase translated 'for ever and ever' (*eis tous aiōnas* or *eis tous aiōnas ton aiōnon*) 'is consistently the most emphatic way of saying "forever" in the New Testament'. Hence it cannot be explained away by descriptions, such as that suggested by David Powys, which reduce it to a 'figurative' expression whose force derives from 'the immediacy and the terror of the threat of persecution and . . . the depth of division and resentment caused by apostasy'.[27] Moreover, John's vision of the apostates being deprived of rest 'day and night' is taken by traditionalists as further evidence that divine retribution must be endless.[28] Guillebaud, however, anticipates this deduction

---

24. Wenham, 'Conditional Immortality', pp. 179–80; Fudge, *Fire*, pp. 187–9; Stott, *Essentials*, p. 316.
25. 'New Testament Teaching', p. 215.
26. Wenham, 'Conditional Immortality', p. 180.
27. Carson, *Gagging of God*, pp. 525–6; Powys, *Hard Look*, p. 367.
28. Carson, *Gagging of God*, pp. 525–6; Peterson, *Hell on Trial*, p. 88.

and retorts that although 'day and night' here might well imply *continuous* suffering, it does not necessarily imply *everlasting* suffering. Hence from his point of view these words imply that there will be 'no break or intermission in the suffering of the followers of the Beast, while it continues; but in themselves they do not say that it will continue forever'.[29] In other words, however sustained and dreadful the punishment here may be, we can still read it as one day coming to a close.

Guillebaud's 'continuous but conclusive' view of divine retribution in Revelation 14:11 has proved attractive to other conditionalists,[30] but it is challenged by the language of another crucial verse from the Apocalypse – namely Revelation 20:10. Here, John reports that the devil, the beast and the false prophet are 'tormented' not only 'day and night' *but also* 'forever and ever'. Although the conjunction of these two phrases might suggest that the duration of the apostates' agony in Revelation 14:11 is similarly eternal, Stott notes that this is the only such conjunction in the New Testament, and that in any case the referents here are different. Indeed, he argues that 'the devil, the beast and the false prophet' cannot be equated with people, and that in this context they more probably function as 'symbols of the world in its varied hostility to God', in which case they could not realistically be said to experience pain. Michael Green follows a similar explanation, maintaining that this isolated verse is not enough on which to build what he calls the 'savage doctrine' of eternal human suffering.[31] These premises lead Stott to conclude that 'the most natural way to understand the reality behind the imagery is that ultimately all enmity and resistance to God will be destroyed. So both the language of destruction and the imagery of fire seem to point to annihilation.'[32] As backing

---

29. Guillebaud, *Righteous Judge*, p. 24. This argument is taken up by Fudge, *Fire*, pp. 189–90.

30. See, for instance, Fudge, *Fire*, pp. 189–90; Froom, *Conditionalist Faith (Vol 1)*, pp. 298, 301, 409.

31. Stott, *Essentials*, p. 318.; Green, Michael, *Evangelism Through The Local Church*, London: Hodder & Stoughton, 1990, p. 70.

32. Stott, *Essentials*, p. 318.

for this, he emphasises that the 'harlot Babylon' and 'Death and Hades', which are clearly impersonal, *also* get cast into the fire (Rev. 18:7.10.15; 20:13–14). Fudge, Pinnock and Wenham see the sense of termination and finality here further summed up in v.14, where the lake of fire is defined as 'the second death'. This they take to be a clear reference to annihilation, and to the absolute extinction of all the 'death, mourning, crying and pain' which is said to have come to an end by Revelation 21:4.[33]

Traditionalists have responded to this 'symbolic' reading in various ways. First, Pawson, turning the conditionalist argument on its head, asserts that the devil and his henchmen *are* personal beings. Otherwise, he asks, why would they be ascribed the very personal quality of 'torment'?[34] Besides, in the parable of the sheep and the goats (Matt. 25:31–46), the goats (who clearly represent unrighteous humans) are 'not only sent to the same *place* as the devil and his angels, but into the same *punishment*, which is eternal'.[35] Peter Cotterell makes a similar point and goes on to assert that the semantic yoking of 'day and night' with 'forever' here cannot be dismissed simply 'on the grounds that [it] is so stated only once'. Rather, he sees it as a stock phrase which *can* legitimately be taken to inform our understanding of what happens to the reprobate.[36] As for the casting of 'death and Hades' into the fiery lake and the description of the lake itself as the 'second death', Peterson voices a familiar traditionalist response when he argues that these need no more signify an end of individual *existence* than the 'first death' does:

> As death means the separation of the soul from the body, so the second death denotes the ultimate separation of the ungodly from their Creator's love. Accordingly, God reunites the souls of the unsaved dead with their bodies to fit

---

33. Fudge, *Fire*, pp. 193–94; Pinnock, Clark H. 'Fire then Nothing', *Christianity Today*. 20th March 1987; Wenham, John, *The Goodness of God*, Leicester: IVP, 1974, p. 78.

34. Pawson, *Road to Hell*, p. 42 & pp. 150ff.

35. Pawson, *Road to Hell*, p. 164.

36. Cotterell, Peter, *Mission and Meaninglessness*, London: SPCK, 1990, p. 73.

the lost for eternal punishment. If eternal life entails forever knowing the Father and the Son (John 17:3), its antithesis, the second death, involves being deprived of God's fellowship for all eternity.[37]

More specifically, John Blanchard contends that 'death' in Scripture never equates to annihilation, and is frequently used to describe the condition of those who *continue* to exist in estrangement from God (as in Matt. 8:22; 1 Tim. 5:6; Jas. 2:26). He adds that the 'lake of fire' here linked to 'the second death' has already been defined as an instrument of 'eternal torment' in v. 10, and is unlikely to have changed its function a few sentences later. Moreover, writes Blanchard, in Revelation 2:11 the Church in Smyrna is assured that Christians who overcome persecution 'will not be hurt at all by the second death' – an assurance which implies that the same 'second death' must involve pain and suffering rather than mere extinction.[38]

As we have hinted, even where conditionalists concede that the precise meaning of the 'second death' may be open to question, they regularly go on to point out that Revelation 21 begins with a cosmic re-creation in which suffering of *all* kinds is banished from *every part* of God's 'new universe', and in which the agonies of hell must thereby logically 'pass away' along with 'the old order of things' (21:1–4). Pinnock and Brow put this case succinctly:

> Surely in the end God will be completely victorious over sin and death, suffering and Satan. Only if all of them go up in smoke does history end in the unqualified victory of God. According to the traditional view, darkness will hang over the new creation forever. It makes better sense metaphysically to think of hell as final destruction and the dwindling out of existence of the impenitent wicked than to posit the eternal existence alongside God of a disloyal opposition in an unredeemed corner of the new creation. What sort of new creation would that be?[39]

---

37. Peterson, *Hell on Trial*, p. 90.
38. *Whatever*, pp. 227–8.
39. *Unbounded Love*, pp. 87–95. Similar cosmological arguments are adduced by Powys, *Hard Look*, pp. 368–78 and Ellis, 'New Testament Teaching', pp. 216–7.

Undeterred by such reasoning, however, traditionalists are quick to counter that one has only to read on a little to find various impenitent sinners still immersed in the fiery lake and still undergoing the 'second death' (21:8). Furthermore, even if the tense-structures here allow that this might be interpreted as a 'glance backwards' to the final judgment, there is a further suggestion of unceasing conscious retribution in 22:15, with its portrayal of 'the dogs' – that is, occultists, sexual offenders, murderers and 'all who love and practise falsehood' – exiled outside the gates of the New Jerusalem. For Peterson this clearly means that there *must* be some part of the final order reserved for the unrighteous.[40]

From the conditionalist viewpoint, David Powys acknowledges this argument and admits the genuine problems presented by Revelation 22:15. Even so, he insists that it should be set alongside 22:3, which states that 'everything cursed will be no longer', and 22:14, which indicates that the 'dogs' will be barred from 'the tree of life'. His deduction is that, even if such unrighteous persons remained in existence for a time, 'they would not remain so for long'. Specifically, v. 14 may be alluding to 'another way of regarding their fate: not as precipitative annihilation but rather as death caused by lack of access to the Source of Life, that Source being epitomised by the tree of life'.[41] This accords with Pinnock and Brow's picture (quoted above) of the impenitent wicked 'dwindling out of existence'.

The Order of Condemnation

A more general traditionalist objection to conditionalist apocalyptic is that it imposes a retrospective *sequencing* on the events described in Scripture – one that is not justified by the

---

40. Peterson, *Hell on Trial*, p. 92. The same line is taken by Packer, *Eternal Punishment*, p. 13. For a fuller consideration of this issue of the 'view from heaven', see Blanchard, *Whatever*, pp. 179–81.

41. Powys, *Hard Look*, pp. 373–4.

relevant texts as they stand. Kendall Harmon states this objection as follows:

> For Fudge, God's final sentence *begins* with banishment, *continues* with a period of conscious suffering, and *ends* with destruction. In fact, not a single New Testament passage teaches exactly this sequence. Instead, some texts speak of personal exclusion, some of punishment, and others of destruction, and these images need to be understood as giving us hints at the same eschatological reality. Fudge not only chronologizes these images, but he also emphasises one to the exclusion of the other two: destruction dominates while punishment and exclusion fall into the background. Indeed, the latter image is hardly discussed. (Emphases original).[42]

Fudge's own response to this is to assert that Harmon himself accepts exclusion, conscious punishment and destruction as the 'dominant themes' of the Bible's teaching on hell, and that if this is the case it would be hard to conceive any other logical sequence for them:

> Is not 'exclusion' the first step in any scenario? If 'destruction' really means what it sounds like, how can anything else follow after it? The truth is that the traditional position is forced to define 'death', 'destruction' and 'corruption' alike as 'eternal existence under painful circumstances'. It is that definition, not some exegetical error on my part, which requires anyone to reject the simple order I suggest.[43]

Other Images Related to Hell

There are several other biblical texts and recurrent images which contribute to the understanding of hell. From Jesus' dialogue with the faithful centurion (Matt. 8:11), from the parable of the wedding banquet (Matt. 22:13) and from the letter of Jude (13) we see those condemned at judgment being consigned to a realm of 'darkness', which Jesus also describes as a place of weeping and gnashing teeth. From 2 Thessalonians

---

42. Harmon, 'Case against Conditionalism', p. 213. Carson makes the same point: *Gagging of God*, pp. 525–6.
43. *Fire*, p. 190 n.47.

1:9 we derive a vivid sense of hell comprising irreversible separation from God. And from Revelation 16:19, 18:6 and 19:15, we see the unrighteous condemned to taste the 'cup of God's wrath' – a destiny which entails extreme fear, grief, mourning and famine. While all these descriptions reinforce the sheer awfulness of hell, they do not *in themselves* impinge directly on the traditionalist/conditionalist debate. Since it is this that concerns us chiefly here, we simply note them and move on to problems more usually treated under the aegis of dogmatic and systematic theology.[44]

A Second Chance After Death?

One of the greatest challenges to the traditional understanding of hell is the problem of those who die without having heard the gospel. Although this is a soteriological and missiological problem which is distinct from our main focus on the nature of hell itself, it does relate to questions about what hell is and whom it is for.

Many theologians are inclined to see salvation extended to those who die without having heard the gospel, but recognise that this poses problems for human freedom which are similar to those presented by universalism. Some have derived a solution to this dilemma from 1 Peter 3:18–20 and 4:6, where Jesus is shown preaching to 'the spirits in prison who disobeyed long ago' and to 'those who are now dead, that they might be judged according to human standards in regard to the body, but live according to God in regard to the spirit'.

At least since the work of Origen in the third century, these Petrine texts have been taken to teach what has variously been called a 'Hades Gospel', 'Second Probation' and 'Post-Mortem Salvation'. The inference drawn from them is that God will

---

44. For representative exegeses of these texts see relevant discussions in Fudge, *Fire*; Powys, *Hard Look* (Conditionalist) and Blanchard, *Whatever*; Peterson, *Hell on Trial* (Traditionalist).

offer a 'second chance' for some or all unbelievers to respond to his grace after they have died. In fact, since the emphasis here is really on the *opportunity of the unbeliever to receive Christ*, this view would be more accurately described as 'post-mortem repentance'. While there are certain similarities here with the doctrine of purgatory, most recent advocates of post-mortem repentance have been Protestants who disavow the extended remedial process associated with purgatory, and present the 'second chance' as a more benevolent view of final judgment. Hence Clark Pinnock follows Wolfhart Pannenberg, C.E.B. Cranfield and G.R. Beasley-Murray when he deems it plausible to suppose that for Peter 'the gospel comes to the dead so that they "might live in the spirit with God" if they respond to the proclamation they hear'.[45]

Pinnock traces a link in all this to Jesus' own 'descent into hell', as inferred from Acts 2:31 and Ephesians 4:9–10 by early church fathers like Clement of Alexandria, Athanasius and Jerome, and as affirmed in the Apostles' Creed. Certainly, Melito, Gregory of Nazianzus and Ephraem made quite explicit connections between this *descensus* and Christ's rescue of all but the wickedest souls in Hades.[46] Like them, Pinnock argues that Jesus in this way 'triumphs over Satan by taking away from him even those whom the enemy thought were securely his'. People who through no fault of their own never came into contact with the gospel can have 'a part in its benefits by the extraordinary grace of God'. For Pinnock, this

---

45. Pinnock, Clark, 'The Finality of Jesus Christ in a World of Religions', in Noll, Mark A. and Wells, David F. (eds.), *Christian Faith and Practice in the Modern World: Theology from an Evangelical Point of View*, Grand Rapids: Eerdmans, 1988, pp. 165–6.

46. For more on the development of Patristic views of the *descensus* and its relation to post-mortem salvation see Du Toit, D.A., 'Descensus and Universalism: Some Historical Patterns of Interpretation', in Cameron, Nigel M. de S. (ed.), *Universalism and the Doctrine of Hell*, pp. 73–92; Evans, Stephen T., *Risen Indeed: A Christian Philosophy of Resurrection*, Grand Rapids: Eerdmans, 1993, pp. 159–65; Bloesch, D.G., 'Descent into Hell (Hades)' in Elwell, Walter A. (ed.), *Evangelical Dictionary of Theology*, Exeter: Paternoster, 1984, pp. 313–5.

interpretation makes good 'the universal reach of atonement and the divine willingness that all should know it'.[47]

Another recent advocate of post-mortem repentance is the self-styled 'radical evangelical' Nigel Wright:

> The key question, therefore, is not so much whether human beings can be redeemed beyond death as whether God's search for his fallen creatures is thwarted by death or continues beyond it. The judge of the earth will certainly do right, but from the perspective we currently occupy it is reasonable to suppose that this includes a universal search to win human beings to relationship with himself which does not cease at the point of human death. By this point some people might well have excluded themselves from the divine life, but we can not assume that in every case. Neither should we assume that 'post-mortem' evangelism must necessarily lead to universal salvation, as though people find it easier to believe once confronted beyond death with the living God.[48]

However understandable the moral and philosophical motivation of this argument, it is seriously lacking in exegetical foundation. Indeed, it has been rejected on this basis not only by traditionalists, but also by the majority of evangelical conditionalists. In fact, drawing on similar material in the Book of Enoch, New Testament scholars now generally take the 'spirits' of 3:19 to be just that – spirits, and more specifically, fallen angelic spirits incarcerated at the time of Jesus' resurrection.[49] Hence Powys convincingly shows that 1 Peter 3:19 offers no evidence of post-mortem repentance. Rather, he locates it as a necessary proclamation of Jesus' authority to those 'angels, authorities, and powers subject to him' – a proclamation made prior to his ascension. Furthermore, there is no real indication in the text that these spirits were shamed by this proclamation, or that it led to any kind of repentance or

47. Pinnock, 'Finality', p. 166.
48. *Radical Evangelical*, p. 99.
49. Frame, J.M., 'Second Chance', in Elwell, Walter A., *Evangelical Dictionary of Theology*, Exeter: Paternoster, 1984, pp. 991–2; France, R.T., 'Exegesis in Practice: Two Samples', in I.H. Marshall (ed.), *New Testament Interpretation*, Exeter: Paternoster, 1977, pp. 264–81. For further detail and contemporary references on this text see Powys, *Hard Look.*, pp. 400–11.

redemption. Indeed, Fudge underlines that the completed, historical orientation of the verse suggests that even if Peter *is* referring to human beings, he says 'nothing about the situation beyond the judgment, nor does [he] mention a second chance or offer of salvation beyond the present life'.[50]

As for 1 Peter 4:6, it is most likely that this also refers to the past proclamation of Christ, rather than to any ongoing declaration of the gospel by him to those who die without hearing the gospel. The 'dead' here are most probably either those who were 'dead to sin' until they heard Christ preaching in his earthly ministry, or those who heard him and then went on to die as martyrs.[51]

Quite apart from these specific textual problems, post-mortem redemption undermines the more general biblical principle which we established in Chapter 2, that death represents a decisive and irrevocable step to final judgment (Luke 16:9–31; John 8:24; Heb. 9:27). In addition, it appears to neglect the point that no human being is entitled *as a matter of right* to receive salvation, but is granted it only by the sheer, unmerited grace of God, which releases us from our universal condemnation in Adam (Rom. 3:23; 5:12–17).

While 'second chance' teaching may be hermeneutically flawed, we do nonetheless recognise that it springs from a commendable motive – that is, the desire to see as many people as possible in heaven. Of course, we recognise that this desire must be set alongside the biblical doctrines of election and predestination, and Jesus' warnings about the narrow and broad paths, the many and the few (Matt. 7:13, cf. Matt. 22:14). We also acknowledge that the final number and identity of the saved can be known only to God. Even so, we pray earnestly for evangelistic and missionary efforts motivated by the conviction that God desires all people of every nation to gain eternal life through hearing the gospel and trusting in Christ (Matt. 28:19; 1 Tim. 2:3–4).

---

50. Powys, *Hard Look*, p. 401; Fudge, *Fire*, p. 201.
51. Powys, *Hard Look*, pp. 401–3.

A Wider Hope? Old Testament Saints, the Unevangelized, Infants and the Mentally Disabled

Although Scripture lends no real support to the idea that unbelievers might get a second chance to *repent* after death, it does appear to widen the scope of God's sovereign *redemption* beyond overtly committed disciples of Christ – albeit in quite specific cases. The first such case is that of the faithful children of Old Covenant Israel, several of whom are identified as spiritual heroes and heroines in Hebrews 11. Here, it is made quite clear that faith was a prerequisite of their salvation, but that as far as Jesus Christ is concerned, this faith was implicit: 'they did not receive the things promised; they only saw them and welcomed them from a distance' (11:13). Although this confirms that salvation is not confined to Christians, it is clear that the conditions invoked apply specifically to the period before the incarnation.

As far as the Christian era is concerned, a second model of 'implicit faith' can be inferred from Romans 2:12–16. Here Paul appears to suggest that it is possible for unbelieving Gentiles who 'do not have the law' to be judged according to their innate moral understanding, or 'conscience'. Specifically, he sees them being approved or condemned according to how they have responded to natural law and the general revelation of God in nature. A case can be made for extrapolating from this to a 'wider hope' for all today who do not hear the gospel before they die. As Romans unfolds, however, it becomes plain that Jesus Christ has rendered the law less central than it was under the old dispensation, and that this has in turn made hearing and responding to the gospel a matter of critical importance (Rom. 10:12–17). In any case, it would be wrong to rely on the vagaries of conscience, which is itself affected by sin and thus hardly an infallible guide into eternal life. Hence, speculation about whether God will redeem some or all of 'those who have not heard' should not detract from our presentation of Christ as the only way to salvation.

The third case in which God may receive some who have not professed faith concerns those who die in infancy. This can be a devastating experience for family and friends, and must be handled with great compassion. Scripture provides no explicit teaching on this matter, but it does offer hints that some or even all of those who die before they are old enough to make a conscious commitment, might be saved. Given that the indwelling of the Holy Spirit is a mark of regeneration, it may be significant in this regard that John the Baptist was 'filled with the Spirit, *even from his mother's womb*' (Luke 1:15). Jesus himself presented the kingdom of God as belonging to children (Matt. 19:13–15), and urged adults to enter that kingdom like a child (Luke 18:15–17).[52] None of this should be taken to support the view that children are inherently innocent; on the contrary, Psalm 51:5 confirms that we are born in iniquity and 'conceived in sin'. As Ronald Nash has pointed out, however, our final judgment as individuals is conducted on the basis not of our sinful *condition* as members of a fallen human race, but on the basis of the sinful *deeds* we commit 'in the body' (2 Cor. 5:10).[53] By definition, this standard cannot apply to deceased infants. Nash sees in this a premise for arguing that *all* who die in infancy should be numbered among the elect, and Lorraine Boettner has pointed out in striking terms that this in itself would ensure that the population of heaven comprised over 50% of all who have ever lived![54] Others have taken a more cautious line which sees a special grace being extended to the offspring of believers, but which remains agnostic about the destiny of the rest (cf. Gen. 7:1; Josh. 2:18; Ps. 103:17; John 4:53; Acts 2:39; 16:31; 18:8; 1 Cor. 1:16; 7:14; Titus 1:6).[55]

---

52. For more detail on this subject, and the texts cited in this regard, see Nash, Ronald H., *When A Baby Dies: Answers to Comfort Grieving Parents*, Grand Rapids: Zondervan, 1999; Grudem, Wayne, *Systematic Theology*, Leicester: IVP, 1994, pp. 499–501; Blanchard, *Whatever*, pp. 254–255.

53. *When A Baby Dies*, pp. 60–65.

54. Boettner, Lorraine, *The Reformed Doctrine of Predestination*, Presbyterian and Reformed Publishing Co., 1992, pp. 145–46.

55. E.g. Grudem, Wayne, *Systematic Theology*, Leicester: IVP, 1994, p. 500.

What is clear is that if those who die as infants *are* granted eternal life, it will come through no merit or claim of their own. The same would apply to a fourth category of persons sometimes linked to the 'wider hope' – those whose mental disability renders them unable to respond overtly to the gospel. As with the other groups just discussed, any redemption which might apply here would derive purely from the work of Christ (Rom. 9:14–18). That God in his generosity might make exceptions in these cases should not, however, lead us to base either our evangelistic programmes or our pastoral care on what are, at best, no more than caveats on the Great Commission.

7

The Doctrine of Hell Among Evangelicals Today: III. Key Theological Issues

Theological arguments on the nature and purpose of hell can be treated under four main headings: immortality, love and justice, victory, and the blessedness of the redeemed.

Immortality

We have already noted the biblical grounds on which conditionalists attack the view that human beings have an 'eternal soul'. It should be realised, however, that their critique of traditionalism is made in philosophical as well as exegetical terms. Specifically, they argue that the doctrine of eternal conscious punishment owes more to classical Greek philosophy than it does to scriptural teaching, and that this has in turn produced a flawed moral theology.[1] Pinnock and Brow present this critique with typical forthrightness:

> Why has the annihilationist possibility not been noticed much before? Why would anybody have turned the notion of destruction into everlasting life in hell, creating this monstrous problem? We attribute it to the influence on theology of the Greek idea of the immortality of the soul. With that view entering the picture, the shift is logical and inevitable. If souls are immortal and

---

1. Travis, *Christian Hope*, p. 135.

hell exists, it follows that the wicked will have to suffer consciously forever in it. If the soul is naturally immortal, it has to spend eternity somewhere. If there is a Gehenna of fire, hell has to be a condition of torment. The conclusion flows inexorably from the Greek premise. Thus the word *destruction* gets turned into "everlasting torment". But belief in the immortality of the soul is not a biblical view. The Bible points to a resurrection of the whole person as a gift of God, not a natural possession. Humans were not created with a natural capacity for everlasting life – Jesus Christ brought immortality to light through the gospel (2 Tim. 1:10). The soul is not an immortal substance that has to exist eternally. Let us just accept exactly what Jesus says: God is able to destroy both body and soul in hell (Mt. 10:28). The idea of natural immortality seems to have skewed the Christian teaching about hell. It was a mistake and we should correct it.[2]

Pinnock, Brow and other leading conditionalists follow the thesis expounded by H.A. Wolfson in the 1960s, that Plato's core doctrine of the immortality of the soul, with its corresponding assertion of bodily mortality, was widely 'christianised' in the second and third centuries for reasons of apologetic expedience.[3] Wolfson holds that key early fathers took their cue from the Hellenistic Jewish writer Philo, and then applied Plato's dualism in particular to the resurrection, to make it plausible for their Graeco-Roman audience. Hence final judgment came to be seen as the consignment of discarnate 'eternal souls' to heaven or hell, rather than the divine examination of resurrected human persons. Conditionalists generally proceed from this premise to argue that such 'Platonisation' of biblical anthropology obscured the true scriptural picture, and that once made, the mistake was compounded by the Reformers, and by many of their evangelical successors.[4]

---

2. Pinnock & Brow, *Unbounded Love*, p. 92. For more detailed conditionalist assessment of the philosophical background to this issue see Fudge, *Fire*, pp. 32–40; for a representative traditionalist response see Blanchard, *Whatever*, pp. 68–73, 214–17.

3. Wolfson, H.A., 'Notes on Patristic Philosophy', *Harvard Theological Review* 57, no. 2 (April 1964), p. 124; 'Immortality and Resurrection in the Philosophy of the Church Fathers', in Krister Stendahl (ed.), *Immortality and Resurrection*, New York: Macmillan, 1965.

4. E.g. Fudge, *Fire*, pp. 33–40; Travis, *Christian Hope*, p. 135.

The precise extent of Platonic influence on the church fathers continues to be debated.[5] Even so, most traditionalists have been willing to concede that some did indeed co-opt Platonic anthropology, and that this was at odds with the 'holistic' biblical view of humanity, which promotes an essential integration of body, mind, soul and spirit. Nonetheless, traditionalists maintain that to repudiate Platonic influence here does not undermine the fact that the Bible itself teaches the immortality of men and women. As Fernando puts it, 'if some people [have] obtained their view of the unending existence of persons from the Greek view of human nature, then they have got it from an erroneous source. But they don't need to discard this belief for the Bible also teaches it.'[6] To make this point clearer, Peterson and Blanchard prefer to talk of the 'immortality of man', rather than of the soul alone.[7] Furthermore, they argue that it is this distinctively biblical, holistic form of immortalism which underlies the orthodox tradition of the church. Thus Peterson writes of Tertullian, Augustine, Aquinas, Luther, Calvin and Jonathan Edwards:

> ...it is ludicrous to argue that they held to eternal torment because they were influenced by Platonic philosophy. If we take their own claims seriously, they believed in this terrible doctrine out of fidelity to biblical teaching – sometimes against their own natural inclinations ... their view of immortality was not Platonic but biblical. They did not hold that the souls of humans were inherently immortal, as did Plato. Rather, acknowledging that God 'alone is immortal', as Paul says (1 Tim. 6:16), they taught that the immortal God grants immortality to all human beings.[8]

This exposition is characteristic of the traditionalist view that human immortality is irrevocably conferred by God at creation, rather than being intrinsically possessed by humans, to be retained or forfeited by them at will. There are, however,

---

5. On this whole area see the work of Cooper, J.W., *Body, Soul and the Life Everlasting*, Grand Rapids: Eerdmans, 1989.

6. *Crucial Questions*, p. 43.

7. Peterson, *Hell on Trial*, p. 178; Blanchard, *Whatever*, pp. 214–7.

8. Peterson, *Hell on Trial*, p. 177.

two significant problems with this distinction. The first derives from the obvious point that in biblical terms *every* facet of human personhood is conferred by God, since God created us in all our parts. The distinction is therefore true, but insignificant for the specific debate on hell. The second is that the plain sense, not only of 1 Timothy 6:16, but of similar texts such as 1 Timothy 1:17 and 2 Timothy 1:10, can at least as easily be invoked by conditionalists. They, after all, either assume that humanity was made mortal from the beginning by an immortal God, or see our created immortality cancelled by the sin of Adam and restored only by the redemption of Christ – and then only to believers.[9]

In the face of these complications, Paul Helm acknowledges that human immortality is taught in Scripture implicitly rather than explicitly.[10] However, he is convinced that the corroborative biblical evidence is overwhelming. Pawson and Fernando are similarly confident,[11] while Blanchard sees the doctrine of immortality 'assumed' throughout Scripture in much the same way that the doctrine of the Trinity is assumed without being formally stated. In addition to the Genesis account of man and woman being made 'in the image of God', traditionalists find hints of this doctrine in Ecclesiastes 3:11, with its assertion that God has 'put eternity' into people's hearts, and in Ecclesiastes 12:7, with its assurance that 'the spirit returns to God, who gave it'.[12]

These theological inferences of immortality from the Old Testament may be disputable, but they are nowhere near as contentious as the debates which have arisen around Matthew 10:28 – the text quoted by Pinnock and Brow as the most obvious refutation of eternal conscious punishment in Scripture. Of course, conditionalists would agree with Peterson when he writes that the final state of Christian believers cannot be 'a disembodied spiritual life in heaven, but a holistic

9. Hence John Stott, *Essentials*, p. 316.

10. Helm, Paul, *The Last Things: Death, Judgment, Heaven and Hell*, Edinburgh: Banner Of Truth, 1989, p. 118.

11. Pawson, *Road to Hell*, pp. 94ff.; Fernando, Ajith, *Crucial Questions*, pp. 42–3.

12. Blanchard, *Whatever*, pp. 215–6.

resurrected one on the new earth'.[13] True as this is, however, it
fails to address Pinnock and Brow's point about the destruction
of unbelievers' 'souls and bodies' in hell. The most Peterson
offers on this is a comparison with Luke 12:5, in which he
simply takes 'bodily destruction' to be a figurative synonym for
'being thrown into hell'. The problem is that even this exegesis
overlooks the Lucan version's image of the body being 'killed'
before it is cast into Hades. This raises the question of precisely
what aspects of the existence of unredeemed people continue
after judgment, even if we make the traditionalist assumption
that the existence of such unredeemed people is eternal.

At this point, traditionalists diverge among themselves.
Some are prepared on the basis of these texts to countenance a
purely 'spiritual' eternity for the damned – one in which they
continue in a literally 'soul-less', dis-integrated travesty of the
whole persons God meant them to be – 'existing' forever
without truly 'living'. Pawson hints at this when he notes that
the word translated 'destruction' (*apollymi*) in Matthew 10:28
can also mean 'wasted' or 'ruined'. Pawson remarks that
'continued existence in a ruined condition would certainly be
much more terrifying than the death of the body'. Although
perplexed as to why God would 'clothe' deceased people in a
new resurrection body only to destroy that body after judgment, Pawson admits that this is a purely speculative question,
leaving open the possibility of an eternal torment which is
discarnate and tragically sub-human.[14] It is this possibility, in
fact, which forms the basis of C.S. Lewis's *The Great Divorce*, in
which those condemned to hell subsist as shadowy 'ghosts'
devoid of either material substance or true personhood.[15]
Although Lewis differed from the traditionalist evangelical
view in certain other respects (e.g. on purgatory and
post-mortem salvation), his explanation of endless torment
is compelling, and has since proved influential:

---

13. *Hell on Trial*, p. 178.
14. *Road to Hell*, pp. 96–7.
15. *The Great Divorce*, Glasgow: Fontana, 1972 [1946].

... people often talk as if the 'annihilation' of a soul were intrinsically possible. In all our experience, however, the destruction of one thing means the emergence of something else. Burn a log, and you have gases, heat and ash. To *have been* a log means now being those three things. If souls can be destroyed, must there not be a state of *having been* a soul? And is not that, perhaps, the state which is equally well described as torment, destruction, and privation? You will remember that in the parable [of the sheep and the goats, Matt. 25:34ff.] the saved go to a place prepared *for them*, while the damned go to a place never prepared for men at all [i.e. the 'eternal fire prepared for the devil and his angels']. To enter heaven is to become more human than you ever succeeded in being on earth; to enter hell, is to be banished from humanity. What is cast (or casts itself!) into hell is not a man: it is 'remains'. To be a complete man means to have the passions obedient to the will and the will offered to God: to have been a man – to be an ex-man or 'damned ghost' – would presumably mean to consist of a will utterly centred on its self and passions utterly uncontrolled by the will. It is, of course, impossible to imagine what the consciousness of such a creature – already a loose congeries of mutually antagonistic sins rather than a sinner – would be like. There may be a truth in saying that 'hell is hell, not from its own point of view but from the heavenly point of view'. I do not think this belies the severity of Our Lord's words. It is only to the damned that their fate could ever seem less than unendurable.[16]

---

16. Lewis, C.S., *The Problem of Pain*, Glasgow: Fount, 1977 [1940], p. 100. Carson accepts this explanation of the fate of the damned as 'possible', but cautions that it leaves the biblical texts 'a long way behind' (*Gagging of God*, pp. 531–2). In truth, however, it is no less biblical than the more common traditionalist assumption that those who have been condemned at the final judgment maintain an anthropology identical to those who live on in heaven. Notwithstanding Stott's reading of the beast and the false prophet as symbols, the 'sentient' eternal suffering of the devil in the lake of fire (Rev. 20:10–15) may lead us to deduce that condemned humans will also suffer 'sentiently' on the basis that they will be consigned to the same place (Matt. 25:41). (Stott, *Essentials*, p. 318, cf. Carson, *Gagging of God*, p. 527). But no one could seriously argue that Satan's being is the same as that of humans – even of eternally condemned humans! There is therefore no reason to suppose that his 'sentience' will be the same as that of the damned, or that he will experience the pain of hell as they will. Granted, we have seen that 'bodily' images are used to convey the anguish of those who have been condemned (thirsty mouths, weeping eyes, gnashing teeth etc.), but these may well be parabolic analogies for that pain, rather than literal representations of it. Lewis, at least, is prepared to envisage the reprobate as still recognisably human in *appearance* if not in *substance*, but pictures them gradually diminishing and fading from view (*The Great Divorce*, Glasgow: Fontana, 1946, pp. 99ff.). Again this is speculative, but then so are most attempts to define the precise physical and psychical attributes of the damned.

Similar appeals to the conservation of energy and matter have featured in the traditionalist apologetics offered by Blanchard and others.[17] Such appeals show how modern scientific insights can inform long-standing doctrines rather than simply challenging them, although in this case, there are still questions as to whether the original premise of the doctrine is valid. However much the laws of the universe *as they stand* appear to support the eternal existence of the unrighteous in hell, conditionalists could well reply that God is not bound by these laws and may well suspend or revoke them as he 'makes all things new' at the end of the age. In any case, it is clear that purely physical or mechanical analyses of the likely duration of divine punishment are of themselves inadequate and often hypothetical. Moral and ethical categories must also play their part.

Love and Justice

The subject of hell frequently raises questions about God's love and justice. This questioning often packs a strong emotional punch. Given the undeniable terror and gruesomeness with which hell is portrayed in Scripture, even those who reject universalism are prompted to ask what useful *purpose* could be served by God's sustaining the unrighteous in continual torment.

This question is regularly cited by conditionalists as a starting-point for their own abandonment of the traditional position. Thus Stephen Travis argues that the concept of unbelievers being tortured unendingly by their Creator suggests a 'vindictiveness' which is 'incompatible with the love of God in Christ'.[18] Similarly, John Wenham confesses that 'whatever anyone says, unending torment speaks to me of sadism, not justice'.[19] Similar sentiments are declared by

---

17. Blanchard, *Whatever*, pp. 68–9.

18. An argument mooted by John Baillie and taken up by Stephen Travis, *Christian Hope*, p. 135.

19. Wenham, 'Conditional Immortality', p. 187.

Pinnock, Brow, Stott and Wright.[20] The argument in each case is a forceful one: it asks what love and justice could possibly be manifested in everlasting, unrelenting conscious torment, and responds that there is surely a grave disproportion between crimes committed in a single lifetime, and punishment administered for all eternity. As Stott puts it, the belief that people will be judged 'according to what they have done' is fundamental to biblical eschatology, and implies that the penalty imposed by God will be commensurate with the evil they have perpetrated in their earthly life (cf. Rev. 20:12). 'This principle', he continues, 'had been applied in the Jewish law courts, in which penalties were limited to an exact retribution, "life for life, eye for eye, tooth for tooth, hand for hand, foot for foot" (e.g. Ex. 21:23–25). Would there not, then, be a serious imbalance between sins consciously committed in time and torment consciously experienced throughout eternity?'[21]

Traditionalists answer this case by making a distinction between sins committed against other, finite human beings and sins committed against an infinite and perfectly holy God. Peterson, for instance, contends that divine retribution very often appears to be far in excess of that which we might mete out ourselves – whether God is turning Lot's wife to stone for glancing back at Sodom and Gomorrah (Gen. 19:26), striking Uzzah dead for touching the ark (2 Sam. 6:6–7) or slaying Ananias and Sapphira for lying (Acts 5:1–10). For Peterson the rationale for this disproportion remains as it was expressed by Thomas Aquinas in the thirteenth century:

> Now a sin that is against God is infinite; the higher the person against whom it is committed, the graver the sin – it is more criminal to strike a head of state than a private citizen – and God is of infinite greatness. Therefore an infinite punishment is deserved for a sin committed against him.[22]

---

20. Pinnock & Brow, *Unbounded Love*, pp. 89–90; Stott, *Essentials*, p. 314; Wright, *Radical Evangelical*, p. 89.

21. *Essentials*, p. 318.

22. Peterson, *Hell on Trial*, pp. 170–4; *Summa Theologiae*, Blackfriars. New York: McGraw-Hill, 1974, Ia2ae. 87,4.

Although this argument has a neat internal logic, more than one conditionalist has challenged it by emphasising that Christ's atonement on Golgotha was achieved by a finite event at a specific place, and yet had both eternal and cosmic effect in the defeat of sin. If the punishment he bore on the cross for the iniquities of the whole world was limited in time, the argument runs, why does the punishment of mere individual sinners have to be everlasting? Traditionalists have tended to respond by stating that the death of Christ was a one-off occurrence which cannot be used as an analogy for eternal conscious punishment after final judgment.[23] This divergence confirms that questions of hell are never far from questions of soteriology – that is, the doctrine of salvation and theories of atonement. Although detailed explorations of this link lie beyond our remit here, we believe it to be an important and fertile area for further research.

A further response made by traditionalists to the charge of 'disproportionality' is that God alone must be allowed to determine what punishments are appropriate and what are not. Harold Brown puts this clearly when he underlines that 'human concepts of justice and equity, distorted as they are by the sinfulness of fallen human nature, are deceptive and unreliable, and in any case are not binding upon God, who tells us explicitly: "For my thoughts are not your thoughts, neither are your ways my ways" (Is. 55:8).'[24] While most evangelical conditionalists accept this point in principle, they prefer to stress that God's 'ways' should ultimately be seen as more merciful and compassionate than our ways.[25] Nigel Wright, for example, draws this inference chiefly from the decisive revelation of God's character in Jesus:

> If the only God who exists is the Christlike God who loves his enemies, the Father of Jesus Christ, it becomes impossible to believe in an inscrutable,

---

23. For detailed argument and references on this point see Fudge, *Fire*, pp. 17, 135–45.

24. 'Will the Lost Suffer Forever?', *Criswell Theological Review*, 4.2 (1990), p. 272.

25. E.g. Wenham, 'Case for Conditional Immortality', p. 185.

hidden God who is other than what we see in Christ. Jesus did not deny the human sense of love and justice and its potential as an analogy for imaging God. He argued that God was so much more loving and more just than that. So: 'If you, then, though you are evil, know how to give good gifts to your children, *how much more* will your Father in heaven give good gifts to those who ask him!' God's standards of justice and fairness are not less than the human, but so much more.[26]

By contrast, traditionalists suggest that the good intentions which motivate this argument finally skew it away from the full range of scriptural witness on hell. After all, they point out, the same Jesus depicted by conditionalists like Wright is the One who taught more about the retribution and pain of hell than anyone else in Scripture. Besides, they contend, if God is expected to act up to and beyond our limited human notions of mercy, why does he not simply destroy sinners at the point of death, thereby minimising their discomfort even further?[27] Of course, we have already seen that evangelical conditionalists typically reject such 'immediate extinctionism' on exegetical grounds. But they still face the common traditionalist criticism that they are succumbing to contemporary cultural represen-tations of pain as the ultimate evil to be avoided, when sin against God is in fact a more heinous thing. Gerald Bray voices this criticism sharply when he says that conditionalism shifts the model of hell 'from punishment justly deserved for sins committed to suffering pointlessly prolonged' and thereby proposes a solution which is akin to euthanasia, with all the pitfalls which that implies.[28]

If conditionalists recoil from eternal conscious punishment on the grounds that it seems ultimately wanton and pointless, traditionalists reply that it does have a positive aim – namely, to glorify God as a righteous Judge. Bray again articulates this view concisely: 'If the non-elect have no hope of salvation and God does not want them to suffer unduly, why were they ever

---

26. *Radical Evangelical*, p. 91.

27. Blanchard, *Whatever*, pp. 168ff.; Carson, *Gagging of God*, pp. 530–4.

28. Bray, Gerald, 'Hell: Eternal Punishment or Total Annihilation?', *Evangel* 10:2 (Summer 1992), 23.

created in the first place? Their existence must serve some purpose, and once that is admitted the view that their eternal punishment glorifies the justice of God seems perfectly logical.'[29] With this rationale in view, Stott concedes that the only scenario in which eternal conscious torment might be compatible with divine justice is one in which the impenitent wicked continue to rebel for all eternity. This would then (presumably) serve to emphasise the majesty of God as he continues, in justice, to punish them. John Gerstner explains how this might come about when he argues that, since there is no opportunity for repentance after judgment, and since punishment clearly follows on from judgment, 'justice requires it to go on forever'.[30] In other words, what cannot be repented of cannot be cancelled, and what cannot be cancelled must last eternally.[31] If this logic has a weakness, it is that it rules out from the start the cardinal conditionalist premise that the wages of sin is death (or destruction) rather than endless torment. From a conditionalist viewpoint, therefore, it is a logic which is somewhat circular.

Victory

We have already seen in our discussion of Revelation 20–22 that traditionalists and conditionalists differ on how to square John's eschatological vision of a fully redeemed cosmos with the possible persistence of hell within that cosmos. Putting the conditionalist case, Stephen Travis argues that however long the suffering of the reprobate may last after their judgment, it cannot last forever, since 'eternal torment involves an eternal cosmological dualism, which is impossible to reconcile with

---

29. Bray, Gerald, 'Hell: Eternal Punishment or Total Annihilation?', *Evangel* 10.2 (Summer 1992), p. 23.

30. Gerstner, *Repent or Perish*, pp. 61–2.

31. See Carson, D.A, *How Long O Lord?: Reflections On Suffering And Evil*, Leicester: IVP, 1990, p. 103; see also Dixon, *Other Side*, p. 127.

the conviction that ultimately God will be "all in all" [1 Cor. 15:28]'.[32] This same point is often related by conditionalists to the pervasive biblical theme of God's final triumph and reign. Hence for John Stott, the eternal existence of the impenitent in hell 'would be hard to reconcile with the promises of God's final victory over evil, or with the apparently universalistic texts which speak of Christ drawing all men to himself (John 12:32), and of God uniting all things under Christ's headship (Eph. 1:10), reconciling all things to himself through Christ (Col. 1:20) and bringing every knee to bow to Christ and every tongue to confess his lordship (Phil. 2:10–11), so that in the end God will be "all in all" or "everything to everybody"'.[33] Stott is quick to insist that these texts do not warrant universalist interpretation, since they stand alongside so many others which witness to the 'terrible and eternal reality of hell'. Even so, he is led by them to ask 'how God can in any meaningful sense be called "everything to everybody" while an unspecified number of people still continue in rebellion against him and under his judgment'. His conclusion is that 'it would be easier to hold together the awful reality of hell and the universal reign of God if hell means destruction and the impenitent are no more'.[34]

Traditionalists tend to view all this as an easy way out. For them, hell is not incompatible with God's victory, since, as we saw above, they characteristically take its eternal presence to be a confirmation of God's justice – a permanent reminder of his lordship over all. John Blanchard asserts this view plainly: 'Why', he asks, 'should the promise of God's final victory over evil be inconsistent with the everlasting punishment of the wicked if this is what God has ordained? ... God will be glorified as greatly in hell as he will be in heaven; he will reign as completely in one place as in the other. He is sovereign in

---

32. Travis, *Christian Hope*, p. 135.

33. Stott, *Essentials*, p. 319.

34. Stott, *Essentials*, p. 319. For similar reasoning see Ellis, 'New Testament Teaching', p. 217; Wenham, 'Case for Conditional Immortality', p. 189.

wrath as well as in grace.'[35] Likewise, Paul Helm emphasises that hell 'is not a demonic colony which has gained unilateral independence from God. Because there is full recognition of God's justice [in hell], God's character is vindicated'.[36]

Another more speculative rationale for the continuation of hell in God's 'new order of things' is mooted by Blanchard and elaborated by the evangelical biophysicist Douglas Spanner. This argues that an everlasting hell would actually be 'good news', because it would show that God would never ever compromise with sin, and would thereby put an end to the possibility of sin ever again breaking out *again* and ruining his new creation, as it did in the beginning with Adam and Eve. As Spanner puts it, hell in this scenario would serve as the '*never-definitively ending evidence* that God will tolerate no defiance of his wise and sovereign authority', and would be necessary 'lest the temptation to rebel' occurred once more.[37] Intriguing though this idea may be, conditionalists could retort that its premise of a potential 'second fall' is nowhere attested in Scripture.

The Blessedness of the Redeemed

Debate about the persistence or otherwise of hell also touches on the state of the redeemed in heaven. If hell continues eternally, conditionalists ask, how could those who have been saved live in unalloyed joy, knowing of the torment which would be going on there? Thus John Wenham admits 'failing to see how God and the saints could be in perfect bliss with human beings hopelessly sinning and suffering'.[38] Leaving aside our earlier discussion of whether the damned in fact maintain their identity as 'human beings', Nels Ferré elaborates Wenham's point

---

35. *Whatever*, p. 221.
36. Helm, *Last Things*, pp. 116–7.
37. Blanchard, *Whatever*, p. 221; Spanner, Douglas, 'Is Hell Forever?' *Churchman* 110/2, 1996, p. 120. His emphasis.
38. 'Conditional Immortality', p. 189.

when he contends that 'if eternal hell is real, love is eternally frustrated and heaven is a place of mourning and concern for the lost. Such joy and grief cannot go together ... heaven can only be heaven when it has emptied hell, as surely as love is love and God is God.' The same point is made by Philip Hughes.[39]

From the traditionalist perspective, these arguments are usually met by saying that the very process of redemption itself will erase the 'mourning and concern' which might otherwise be felt by those in heaven. Since such redemption entails the redeemed becoming 'more like God', Blanchard suggests that they will be enabled to 'remember no more' the punishment of the wicked, just as God has the capacity to 'remember no more' what is opposed to him (cf. Jer. 31:34; Rom. 8:29).[40] Similarly, just as the righteous are invited to share their master's happiness in heaven (Matt. 25:21,23), so the happiness of the saints will be total, and need not be marred by the continued existence of hell. Indeed, Blanchard is confident on this basis that they will suffer 'no endless regrets, remorse or sorrow'.[41]

In truth, these same essential points could be made just as forcefully in relation to the painful *memories* which the righteous might harbour for those who have been lost to destruction in the conditionalist view. Presumably, if God wanted to remove all knowledge of the fate of the damned (whether ongoing or not) from the consciousness of the righteous, he could do so. The problem, however, is that Scripture sometimes paints a picture which is rather different from this. We have already noted that in Mark 9:48 Jesus alludes to Isaiah 66:24, with its vision of God's people 'looking upon' those who have rebelled against him – those whose 'worm will not die', whose 'fire will not be quenched' and who will appear 'loathsome' to the eyes. If this is taken to imply that the saved will, in fact, witness the sufferings of the lost, more graphic suggestions of the same thing can be inferred from the Book of

---

39. Ferré, Nels F.S., *The Christian Understanding of God*, London: SCM Press, 1951, p. 237. Hughes, *True Image*, 1989.

40. *Whatever*, p. 180–1.

41. *Whatever*, p. 181.

Revelation. Here not only do the saints, apostles and prophets 'rejoice' over the damnation of Babylon (18:20); they join with all the angels in celebrating the defeat of those who have worshipped the beast (15:2–3a). Indeed, as Walter Wink has pointed out, the same sinners are tormented with fire and brimstone not in some far off corner of the cosmos, but 'in the presence of the holy angels and the Lamb' (Rev. 14:10) – that is, 'right before God's throne'.[42]

Obviously we must be careful with apocalyptic imagery such as this, much of which bears symbolic reference to the Roman Empire, as well as to the end times. Perhaps the most we can conclude is that the bliss of heaven will not in any sense be a *qualified* bliss, and that even if we struggle to understand how exactly God will remove the pain of the righteous for the lost, he will do so more effectively than we can imagine this side of glory.

Summary

Our examination of the current debate on hell has shown evangelical opinion to be significantly divided on both exegetical and theological aspects of the issue. From what we have seen, it has become clear that for the most part evangelical conditionalists do not argue from reason or emotion alone, but are sincerely committed to a view which they regard as more biblically and doctrinally correct than the traditional one. We have also seen, however, that while often respecting these intentions, traditionalists reject the conclusions drawn by such conditionalists. The question remains whether these alternative convictions can co-exist authentically within the parameters of evangelicalism. We shall address this in more depth in Chapter 9, but first we must examine various practical and pastoral challenges presented by the subject of hell.

---

42. Wink, Walter, *Unmasking the Powers*, Philadelphia: Fortress Press, 1986, pp. 39–40.

8

Practical and Pastoral Aspects of the Hell Debate

So far we have examined hell from an exegetical and doctrinal perspective. In doing this we have reflected the emphasis of most evangelical literature on the subject. Indeed, as evangelicals ourselves we affirm that all teaching on what happens after death must be based primarily on Scripture, that it must pay serious regard to the historic creeds and confessions of the church down the centuries, and that it must give particular attention to the theologies of Reformation and post-Reformation Protestantism, since it is these theologies which have most distinctively shaped evangelical belief as we know it today.

At the same time, we are concerned that the recent evangelical debate about hell has produced relatively little in the way of *pastoral* reflection.[1] The 1980s and 1990s have seen evangelical biblical scholars and systematic theologians publish an unprecedented flow of material on hell, but the reality is that most Christians are led to deal with it through their everyday contact with unbelievers, through the death of non-Christian relatives or friends, through participation in outreach projects,

---

1. Notable exceptions are: Dowsett, *Not Fair!*; Smith, Anthony M., *Gateway to Life: Death and Bereavement – Help and Hope Along the Journey,* Leicester: IVP, 1994; Cotterell, Peter, *Dealing with Death: A Christian Perspective,* London: Scripture Union, 1994.

and through the queries of inquisitive children. We are also aware that many pastors, preachers and evangelists struggle to communicate this most difficult of topics in an accessible way. As members of a theological commission representing individuals, local churches and Christian agencies, we believe that it is important to address these more practical concerns.

Evangelical Attitudes to Hell

The first point to be made about the pastoral dimensions of hell relates to *attitude*. Traditionalists and conditionalists alike must recognise that this matter merits deep solemnity and soberness. It is biblically indefensible to ignore or marginalise hell, but neither is it something to be relished. There should be no hint of salaciousness in the way we deal with it. The fate of the lost is something to be mourned, not savoured. There is no warrant for evangelical smugness here.[2] When once asked for a theological exposition of this matter, the prominent American evangelical Francis Schaeffer instead remained silent and wept.[3] C.S. Lewis writes of the prospect that some will not be saved, 'There is no doctrine which I would more willingly remove from Christianity than this, but it has the full support of Scripture and, specially, of our Lord's own words.'[4] This balance of human sensitivity and biblical thoroughness is vital: it guards against cold-heartedness on the one hand and sentimentality on the other.

Hell and Mission

Where evangelicals have responded to the pastoral consequences of teaching on hell, they have most often presented it

---

2. A point made strongly by Stott, *Essentials*, p. 312.
3. Blanchard, *Whatever*, pp. 114–115.
4. Lewis, *Problem of Pain*, p. 94.

as a spur to mission. Knowing the 'terror of the Lord' in this regard has been a primary motive for 'persuading others' (2 Cor. 5:11). It was on this basis that Hudson Taylor contemplated 360 million Chinese souls 'dying ... without any of the consolations of the Gospel' and then pioneered evangelistic work in inland China.[5] Similarly William Booth maintained that if only his Salvation Army officers could spend one night in hell, the power of their mission would be immeasurably strengthened.[6] In Dick Dowsett's terms, 'if we want to take Jesus' teaching seriously, we shall want to make people face their most urgent need of the Saviour'.[7] John Blanchard expresses the same sentiment in the form of a question: 'How can you possibly accept that multitudes of people – including many you know personally – are on a collision course with an announcement of God's righteous and terrifying condemnation and yet do nothing to warn them of their danger?'[8] David Pawson goes so far as to see such neglect as *itself* liable to divine judgment and exclusion – a key means by which followers of Christ could jeopardise their own eternal destiny.[9]

Evangelicals have typically seen hell as a tragic fate from which unbelievers must be rescued, and have often found warrant for this view in Jude's encouragement to 'snatch others from the fire' (Jude 23).[10] Furthermore, they have understood this rescue to be made effective primarily through the proclamation of the gospel. Hence, Romans 10:14–15 has been central in evangelical missiology: 'How then can they call on the one they have not believed in? And how can they hear without someone preaching to them? And how can they preach unless they are sent? As it is written, "How beautiful are

---

5. Cit. Dowsett, *Not Fair!* p. 55.

6. Cit. Dowsett, *Not Fair!* p. 55.

7. *God, That's Not Fair!* p. 63.

8. *Whatever*, p. 292.

9. *Road to Hell*, p. 103.

10. For contemporary examples see Blanchard, *Whatever*, 1983, p. 296; Packer, *Eternal Punishment*, pp. 7, 15; Dowsett, *Not Fair!*, p. 51.

the feet of those who bring good news!" '[11] This challenge is as relevant now as it has ever been. All the same, it must be acknowledged that the general strategy implied by it needs to be translated into specific methodologies, and that the place of hell in Christian witness has become a matter of significant debate among evangelicals.

The vivid imagery deployed by Jonathan Edwards to shock people into faith has sometimes functioned as a stereotype of evangelical preaching, but few evangelicals today would focus so intensely on the precise workings of hell. All the same, the conviction that hell must be a prominent theme of the Church's mission to unbelievers remains strong in evangelical circles – even if that conviction is not always so strongly expressed in practice! Ajith Fernando reflects this when he writes that divine judgment is an indispensable subject of our evangelism, even though it may not be the main one: 'If our hearers don't realise that there is a judgment to come, they may not see the need to be saved and thus not realise the good news. They will say that they prefer to rule their lives and seek to find salvation by their own ways.'[12] Alex Buchanan concurs, and asserts that one of the most important reasons for telling non-Christian people about hell is the fact that Jesus himself did so: 'He is our Master, and we are his servants; so we must heed his injunction: "A student is not above his teacher, but everyone who is fully trained will be like his teacher" (Luke 6:40). Therefore, we must preach the gospel like he did, and preach it as thoroughly as he did.'[13]

This last point may seem obvious, but its premise has recently been questioned by David Pawson, who is as committed to the doctrine of eternal conscious punishment as Buchanan. While accepting that Jesus certainly preached to unbelievers in general terms about the coming judgment of

---

11. For contemporary discussion see Peterson, *Hell on Trial*, p. 229; Blanchard *Whatever*, p. 295.

12. Fernando, *Crucial Questions*, p. 188.

13. Buchanan, Alex, *Heaven and Hell*, Tonbridge: Sovereign World, 1995.

God,[14] Pawson concludes from a close reading of the relevant gospel texts that his more specific warnings about hell were directed to his own disciples, rather than to the unredeemed. This thesis is strongly supported by Pawson's exegesis of Matthew 10:28, Luke 12:4–5, Matthew 25:31–46 and Luke 16:19–31.[15] Pawson infers that Jesus' teaching on hell functioned primarily to alert his own followers to the fate which awaited those who did not receive the gospel, so motivating them to evangelise the lost. In this sense, its orientation is seen as being more directly pastoral and pedagogic than missiological – something that Christians need to understand, but which should not be accorded a central or explicit place in their witness to others. Hence Pawson concludes that 'it is safer for the evangelist to have hell more frequently in his heart than on his lips'.[16] C.S. Lewis goes even further when he warns that in all our discussions of hell 'we should keep steadily before our eyes the possible damnation, not of our enemies nor our friends (since both of these disturb the reason) but of ourselves. This [matter] is not about your wife or your son, nor about Nero or Judas Iscariot; it is about you and me.'[17]

Now Pawson approaches this subject with a wider agenda: to repudiate the Calvinistic doctrine of 'once saved, always saved'. This predisposes him to regard hell as a real prospect for lax Christians as well as for those who have never accepted Christ, and to view it primarily as a subject for consideration within the Church, rather than beyond it. This is not the place to rehearse the Calvinist-Arminian debate, but we acknowledge that Pawson's analysis has shed important new light on the biblical context, and would note that it also reflects the

---

14. *Road to Hell*, p. 77.
15. *Road to Hell*, pp. 91ff. Pawson also acknowledges that the parable of the wedding banquet in Matthew 22:1–14 and Luke 14:15–24 was aimed at Jewish leaders, but sees it as a warning to those who regarded themselves as the 'people of God' not to become complacent, lest they jeopardise their own eternal destiny.
16. *Road to Hell*, pp. 68–69.
17. Lewis, *Problem of Pain*, p. 102.

reality of most evangelical mission work today. Even the Calvinist Dick Dowsett, who staunchly defends the legitimacy of preaching on hell to the unconverted, nonetheless spends most time warning fellow-Christians to maintain hell as a key motive for taking the gospel to all nations.[18]

While the basic idea of hell as a spur to mission unites most traditionalist evangelicals, it is not surprising that the rather different understanding propounded by conditionalists has generated a contrasting emphasis. Nigel Wright, for example, addresses the 'negative' drive of traditionalism in the following terms:

> The motives for mission are greater and richer than this. We engage in mission because the Christian gospel is true, it enables human beings to find liberation and fulfil their destiny, because through it people receive the Spirit of the messianic age and come themselves to participate in his mission of redemption, and because through the gospel people learn how to give glory to God, Father, Son and Spirit. This seems to be enough motivation to be going on with.[19]

Likewise, responding to J.I. Packer's point that conditionalists must inevitably fail to tell the unconverted that their prospects without Christ 'are as bad as they could possibly be',[20] John Wenham writes as follows:

> It seems to me to be a complete fallacy to think that the worse you paint the picture of hell the more effective your evangelism will be ... [T]he God whom I know had compassion on the crowds 'because they were harassed and helpless, like sheep without a shepherd' (Matt. 9:36). He teaches us to think of him as a good earthly father who won't give a snake to a son who asks for a fish (Luke 11:11). 'He knows how we are formed, he remembers that we are dust' (Ps. 103:14) ... I think that the ordinary decent person who is groping his way through life, ignorant of God, battered and perplexed by the sinful world around him, is helped best by introducing him or her to the Jesus of the gospels in his gentleness, truth and power. As we talk, while not hiding the seriousness of sin, we must see that the love of God gets through. To present God [in Packer's terms] as the one whose 'divinely executed retributive process' will

---

18. *Not Fair!*, pp. 141ff..
19. *Radical Evangelical*, p. 100.
20. Packer, *Eternal Punishment*, p. 14.

bring him into everlasting torment unless he believes is hardly likely to help. To any normal way of thinking (and Jesus has told us when we think about God to think how the best of human fathers act), this depicts God as a terrible sadist, not as a loving Father.[21]

Wenham goes on to ask robustly whether John Stott's or Michael Green's conditionalism has made them any less effective as evangelists, and adds that he himself frequently had cause to evangelise others by explaining to them 'the self-destructive power of sin and ... its ultimate power to destroy absolutely'.[22]

There may be some truth in Fernando's assertion that the growth of conditionalist thought in recent times reflects the increasingly 'feelgood', self-esteem-based culture of the contemporary West.[23] However, traditionalists need to remember that the proclamation of the gospel is an invitation to abundant life before it is a warning against eternal damnation (e.g. Matt. 11:28; John 3:16; John 6:35ff.; John 10:10; Rom. 6:23). It is regrettable that so much polarisation has occurred among evangelicals on the question of hell in relation to missionary methods. Surely such methods will best reflect the balance of God's Word when they combine a clear sense of His holiness and justice with an appreciation of His love for the world. Instead of caricaturing each other as the 'hawks' and 'doves' of evangelical eschatology, traditionalists and conditionalists can learn from each other's pastoral inclinations, even if they remain finally unconvinced by their exegesis. As we have seen, neither divine retribution nor Christ's offer of eternal life; neither God's absolute justice nor his gracious mercy; neither images of punishment nor images of destruction in hell, are mutually exclusive in Scripture. In the mission field, as in the seminary, these dual emphases need to be respected.

From this perspective, whether our Christian witness leads us to present judgment in general or hell in particular, we

---

21. Wenham, *Facing Hell*, pp. 249–251.

22. *Facing Hell*, p. 251.

23. *Crucial Questions*, p. 23.

would commend the practical advice of Fernando. He suggests an approach characterised by reasoned and creative argument rather than histrionic oratory; by clear rather than vague definition of the sin which leads to condemnation; by stress on the non-discriminatory nature of both judgment ('*all* have sinned') and salvation ('*all* nations will be blessed'); by the relation of these things to the righteousness of God; by the search for a constructive, Godward response; by the establishment of a larger gospel context, and by a willingness to take opportunities to converse on this area when they arise.[24]

While we can see how all these prerogatives could be upheld by conditionalists as fervently as by traditionalists, we find it difficult to see how the same zeal could attach to advocates of 'second chance' theory, since this would almost certainly encourage Christians to play down the eternal consequences of the missionary encounter. Granted, salvation is the work of God's grace even when it is realised through our ministry. Granted, it does not finally depend on the efficiency of our faith-sharing. Even so, the doctrine of post-mortem repentance runs a very real risk of delegating back to God a responsibility which he has very deliberately assigned to us. Although God may well save some who have not responded explicitly to the gospel, we cannot afford to make this 'wider hope' the basis of our missiology.

Hell and Pastoral Care of the Dying

Pastoral care of the dying throws many of the theological questions we have raised here into sharp relief. What, for example, are we to say to terminally ill patients who have not made a commitment to Christ? Warn them of the fiery flames which await unless they convert, present the gospel's offer of new life and joy everlasting, or both? Clearly, great discernment is needed here. It would be unwise, however, to limit

---

24. *Crucial Questions*, pp. 155–171.

ourselves to one or other position simply for fear of seeming 'unsound', when a different approach may be more faithful to the overall shape and content of biblical teaching.

It is well known that people facing death typically run through a range of emotions including denial, bargaining and acceptance.[25] As they experience these emotions, they are often highly vulnerable. Where such people lack Christian faith, discussion of judgment and hell should be balanced by commendation of the hope of heaven for all who believe. Even here, however, every effort must be made to avoid exploitation and coercion, lest any commitment turn out to have been built on the sand of emotion rather than the rock of genuine conviction. Moreover, Christian doctors are bound by a professional code, which obliges them to respect the existing beliefs of their patients.[26] Nevertheless, regard for the basic rights and freedoms of the individual in this context should not detract from the need of sinners (whether sick or well) for salvation. No doubt certain people will be offended at having the consequences of unbelief presented to them by believing relatives, friends and other visitors to their bedside, and no doubt Christians have sometimes handled such situations very badly. Even so, the fact that our witness may cause offence does not in itself invalidate that witness: however sensitive we are, even in hospital wards and hospices Jesus Christ himself may appear as a stumbling block to some (cf. 1 Cor. 1: 23; 1 Pet. 2:8). It is true that he did not himself confront seriously ill people with teaching on hell, and that he often healed them without preaching or teaching at all (Mark 1:30–31; 5:37–43; 7:31–35; 10:46–52; Luke 5:12–14; 13:10–13). The same is true of certain healings performed by the apostles in the Book of Acts (Acts 9:32–43). But we must not treat miracles like this as a

---

25. Hinton, John, *Dying*, Harmondsworth: Pelican, 1967; Kübler-Ross, Elisabeth, *On Death and Dying*, New York: Macmillan, 1969. From an evangelical perspective see Cotterell, Peter, *Dealing with Death*, London: Scripture Union, 1994; Smith, Anthony M., *Gateway to Life*, Leicester: IVP, 1994.

26. General Medical Council, *Good Medical Practice* (2nd Edn.), London, 1998.

short cut around the presentation of judgment and hell. By
their very nature they are exceptional, and in any case, clear
warnings about God's impending wrath can be found very
early on in the apostolic ministry of words, works and wonders
(Acts 3:23; 17:31).

In all this, we must be wary of viewing a terminally ill
non-Christian patient merely as someone from whom we
need to extract verbal assent to a verbal presentation of the
gospel. It is equally important to reveal the full breadth of
Christ's love to such a patient through practical care, compan-
ionship, touch, and service on behalf of his or her family
(Matt. 22:38; John 13:35).

Hell and Pastoral Care of the Bereaved

The pastoral issues which surround our witness to the dying
are closely related to the care of the bereaved. From a Christian perspective, the funeral or cremation of a believer may
give rise to genuine joy and celebration at the passing of a
fellow-disciple 'from glory to glory'. Even so, it may not be
easy to convey this to relatives and friends who do not themselves profess Christian faith – especially if the believer in
question has died young or unexpectedly. In the short term,
non-Christians' sense of loss may make it difficult for them to
receive the good news of their loved one's eternal rest; this
needs to be understood and respected. In time, however, it
may be that reflection on the deceased Christian's life will
present an opportunity to explain that the God who drew the
sting of death from that person can do the same for those
who mourn.

A greater challenge arises when the person who has died
has remained ambivalent or hostile towards the Christian
faith. All Christians in such circumstances face the problem of
what to say to the bereaved who look for assurance about that
person's eternal destiny. Church leaders bear the added burden of deciding what to preach at the funeral or cremation.

Unfortunately, this is made no easier by the fact that many in these contexts present a universalist stance which avoids most of the issues we have been discussing. Since this is not an option for evangelicals, some way must be found which remains faithful to Scripture while reaching out with compassion to the bereaved.

The first point to make here is that we should not presume upon the sovereign grace and mercy of God. Universalists do this when they purport to know God's hidden will in election by extending salvation to all. But evangelicals are liable to an equal presumption if they assess the eternal fate of a person purely according to their own knowledge of where that person stood in relation to God. No doubt God has revealed the way to salvation as being through Christ, 'the only name under heaven by which people can be saved' (Acts 4:12). Certainly, this salvation is by grace through faith, and not by works of the law (Rom. 11:6). Certainly, we must present commitment to the Son of God as the one enduring hope for a sinful world. But this does not mean that it is given to us to know here and now the exact contents of the Lamb's Book of Life (cf. Rev. 21:27). As a result, it is inadvisable for us to pronounce unequivocally that a specific person is in hell. Rather, we should take the opportunity where possible to affirm the full message of the gospel for those still living: that hell is a clear and present danger for all who refuse Christ, that redemption is guaranteed only in him, and that eternal life can begin now. Beyond this, while it is normal in funeral and cremation liturgies to commend the deceased to the mercy of God and thereby to acknowledge his final authority in judgment, we should resist the temptation to present this as a catch-all exemption clause for unbelievers. As we have already noted, the ultimate fate of non-Christians has in a very real sense already been sealed when their funeral or cremation takes place (cf. Heb. 9:27).

9

Hell and Evangelical Unity

To some extent, the acceptability of both traditionalist and conditionalist views of hell has already been acknowledged within the evangelical constituency. Derek Tidball's influential study of past and present evangelicalism in fact defines this debate as a distinctively evangelical one, which many in the wider church and world would regard as an internal 'family' dispute.[1] Likewise, Rob Warner and Clive Calver's recent account of evangelical unity and doctrine acknowledges conditionalists to be an established 'evangelical party'.[2]

On the other hand, concern has been expressed in certain quarters that conditionalists may be transgressing the boundaries of evangelical orthodoxy. Thus both Anthony Hoekema and John Gerstner provocatively describe the recent growth of evangelical conditionalism as a 'revolt', with Gerstner calling its proponents to repent as a matter of urgency.[3] Then again, evangelical conditionalists can be equally passionate in advocating their own position. Indeed, John Wenham, Clark Pinnock and Robert Brow may fairly be described as

---

1. Tidball, Derek J., *Who Are the Evangelicals?* London: Marshall Pickering, 1994, pp. 152–5.
2. Calver, Clive and Warner, Rob, *Together We Stand: Evangelical Convictions, Unity and Vision*, London: Hodder & Stoughton, 1996, p. 87.
3. Hoekema, *Future*, p. 265; Gerstner, *Repent or Perish*, 1990.

'proselytisers' for the conditionalist cause, seeking to 'convert' evangelicalism from what they regard as a grossly mistaken doctrine of eternal conscious punishment to one which better reflects the true message of the gospel.[4]

In view of such tensions, it is salutary to assess the relative importance of the traditionalist-conditionalist debate for the contemporary evangelical agenda. More specifically, we need to determine those aspects of the doctrine of hell which evangelicals should regard as primary and non-negotiable, as against those aspects which may be deemed *adiaphora* – that is, secondary concerns over which it is possible to differ with integrity.

Of course, the distinction of primary from secondary issues depends to a large degree on how one chooses to define evangelicalism. At present, there is an abundance of studies addressing this matter.[5] All agree that evangelicals are those who believe in a triune God, the incarnation, the sacrificial atonement of Christ, his bodily resurrection and second coming, justification by faith, the supreme authority of the Bible and the missionary prerogative. Yet differences appear when evangelical authenticity is assessed in relation to issues such as baptismal practice, the ecumenical movement, the ordination of women, biblical inerrancy, evolution, spiritual gifts, the millennium and, for that matter, the nature of hell. Some writers see one or more of these issues as 'primary' rather than 'secondary', with lines between essentials and non-essentials being drawn in different places. For others, none of them would warrant separation or breach of fellowship.

---

4. Wenham, 'The Case for Conditional Immortality', p. 190–1; Pinnock & Brow, *Unbounded Love*, pp. 88, 94.

5. Some to mention include: Tidball, Derek, *Who are the Evangelicals?* London: Marshall Pickering, 1994; McGrath, Alister E., *Evangelicalism and the Future of Christianity*, London: Hodder & Stoughton, 1993 and *A Passion for Truth: The Intellectual Coherence of Evangelicalism*, Leicester: Apollos, 1996; Noll, Mark A., *The Scandal of the Evangelical Mind*, Leicester: IVP, 1994; Wells, David F., *No Place for Truth, or Whatever Happened to Evangelical Theology?* Leicester: IVP, 1993; Thompson, Mark, *Saving the Heart: What is an Evangelical?* London: St Matthias Press, 1995.

Furthermore, the actual criteria for determining whether something is primary or secondary for evangelicals are not always straightforward. For our part, we would suggest that they comprise four interrelated considerations. Listed roughly in order of importance these are: a) doctrinal, b) historical, c) ideological and d) relational. It will be useful to apply each of these considerations to the current evangelical debate about hell. This will in turn enable us to draw positive conclusions about the debate, and to make recommendations on how evangelicals should deal with the subject of hell. Since the presenting issue for this report is the acceptability or otherwise of conditionalism, we shall focus our assessment on this in particular.

Conditionalism, Unity and Evangelical Doctrine

The first basis on which evangelicals must establish whether something is either primary or secondary is that of doctrine, and specifically biblical doctrine. The Evangelical Alliance Basis of Faith typifies this priority when it claims as its primary source 'the Scriptures of the Old and New Testaments', and takes these Scriptures to be 'entirely trustworthy' and 'supremely authoritative in all matters of faith and conduct'. Given evangelical agreement on the Bible's witness to the existence of hell *per se*, the question is whether the Bible depicts this hell so unambiguously as a place of eternal torment that no alternative view could legitimately be deemed 'evangelical.'

At the very least, our study has confirmed that the main evangelical proponents of conditionalism demonstrate a high regard for the authority of Scripture, and seek to make their case by thorough exegesis of the relevant texts. In this specific sense, there can be little doubt that they are operating as evangelicals. Furthermore, we would go so far as to say that their work has highlighted verses and images which some traditionalists may previously have ignored or even misconstrued. For instance, no one who has studied the work of Fudge or Powys can seriously read the many biblical references to God's 'destruction' of the impenitent without considering whether they might in fact denote a final cessation of existence rather than endless conscious perishing.

Of course, it must be admitted that a properly evangelical *intention* to uphold the primacy of Scripture does not necessarily lead to proper evangelical theology. As far as possible, evangelicals seek to make doctrine clear and consistent, since they are those who maintain the Reformation principle of biblical 'perspicuity'. On the face of it, this would militate against a conciliatory, 'both/and' approach to conditional immortality/eternal conscious punishment. After all, it seems illogical to suggest that people could be both annihilated and tormented forever! Having said this, it is worth bearing in mind that both conditionalism and traditionalism rely to some extent on words and images from our present space-time world to portray a destiny which lies beyond that world. We now know, however, that space and time are relative even in the present universe, that time is experienced differently at different velocities, and that visibility is affected by gravity. Against this background, Douglas Spanner has suggested intriguingly that one recently discovered feature of the universe may help to resolve the traditionalist–conditionalist dichotomy. A spaceship travelling into a black hole would be sucked in and annihilated. Yet an observer would continue to see this ship appear to hover above the horizon of visibility, gradually fading but without definite end. Similarly, hell might be experienced as annihilation but observed as continuing punishment, gradually fading from view.[6]

Whether or not Spanner's thesis manages to resolve the present evangelical debate, it should be acknowledged that not *every* doctrine need be utterly clear at the present time, or in our current situation. Especially with respect to the last things, certain details of which are hidden from even Christ himself

---

6. Spanner, Douglas, 'Is Hell Forever?' *Churchman* 110/2, 1996, 107–120.

(Mark 13:32), it may be legitimate to accept some divergence of opinion on these details until God discloses them at the end of the age. For instance, evangelicals have accepted different views on the great tribulation of Matthew 24 and Revelation 6–19, while agreeing that it points to an impending reality. Likewise, they can agree on the genuine horror and godless irreversibility of hell, while nonetheless being prepared to wait until judgment day itself to find out whether it will last forever or not.

Conditionalism, Unity and Evangelical History

A second way of distinguishing evangelical essentials from non-essentials is through recourse to history. This approach entails looking back to those periods of the church's life when God has invigorated His people through reformation, revival and renewal. The birth of Protestantism in the early 1500s, the Puritan era and the Evangelical Revival are obvious reference-points here.[7]

Where the doctrine of hell is concerned, this historical criterion of unity is less favourable for conditionalism. After all, evangelicals did not seriously entertain the eventual extinction of the unsaved until the late nineteenth century, and then did so only in relatively small numbers.[8] Besides, it had been consistently anathematised by the Church in the preceding thirteen centuries. At the same time, however, evangelicals are typically cautious about tradition as compared to Scripture, and are wary of appeals to ecclesiastical precedent. One obvious example of the way evangelicals have modified their thinking on a long-established belief is their change of mind on the issue of slavery in the early 1800s. Here was a 'doctrine'

---

7. Alister McGrath makes illuminating use of the Reformers, for example, as one inspiration for evangelicalism today: *Roots that Refresh: A Celebration of Reformation Spirituality*, London: Hodder & Stoughton, 1992.

8. A charge which the work of Seventh Day Adventist L. Froom seeks to demolish, although at times unconvincingly: *Conditionalist Faith*.

and practice which many evangelicals had advocated, and justified from Scripture, but which came to be seen as misguided,
and which evangelicals now would reject out of hand.

As we have seen, some evangelical conditionalists contend
that eternal conscious punishment is at least as deserving of
theological revision as was slavery. What is clear, however, is
that for evangelicals worthy of the name, revision on this or any
other historic article of faith must proceed on the basis of
biblical interpretation rather than mere emotion. Here history
can help, since the interpretative tradition on a biblical text or
doctrine can indicate how heavily the burden of proof lies on
those who wish to change things. In the case of conditionalists
this burden of proof is considerable, since the traditional view
has prevailed for by far the greater part of the Church's history.
It is consequently incumbent upon them to make their case
with humility and respect among traditionalists whose convictions reflect the legacy of Augustine, Calvin, Luther, Wesley,
Edwards and others.

Conditionalism, Unity and Evangelical Ideology

A number of attempts have been made to describe evangelicalism in terms of a particular worldview or ethos. Although
doctrine obviously plays a key part in such definitions, it does
not exhaust them, since they usually embrace more behavioural
features as well. The best known of these ideological
descriptions is the one offered by David Bebbington. This identifies four key characteristics of an evangelical – conversionism
(a call to people to be converted), activism (an active faith affect-
ing all of life), biblicism (a commitment to the authority and
inspiration of the Bible), and crucicentrism (holding the cross at
the centre of all life and theology).[9] If we follow this schema,
those who hold a conditionalist position would remain within
the parameters of authentic evangelicalism. It is clear from the

---

9. Bebbington, *Evangelicalism*.

survey we have conducted that they are certainly committed to conversion and mission, to activism in the world, to the Bible as their ultimate authority, and to the centrality of the cross. By this set of criteria, at least, we would have to conclude that those specific details of hell's duration, quality, finality and purpose which are at issue in the current evangelical debate are comparatively less essential.

Conditionalism, Unity and Evangelical Relationships

Evangelicals often identify one another not because of any clear outward 'badge', but because of what might be called a 'family resemblance'. We are part of the same relational network and, although we may differ from one another in many other ways, we recognise and embrace the differences. Whether we talk of there being various tribes of evangelicals,[10] branches of the same tree,[11] colours of the rainbow, or facets of a Rubik's cube,[12] we tend to know 'family' when we see them. And when it comes to those who have moved from traditionalism towards conditionalism, the familial ties remain strong. They may differ on the details of hell, yet it is clear that virtually all of those who have defended conditionalism recently have done so as self-professed and well-established members of the evangelical household. Some, indeed, have made enormous contributions to it (e.g. John Stott, John Wenham, Michael Green and Philip Hughes).

These images of 'family' and 'tribe' are, of course, also important in Scripture. The people of God, though diverse through time and space, all form part of the same extended community. On this criterion, those who have embraced

10. As in Calver, Clive and Warner, Rob, *Together We Stand: Evangelical Convictions, Unity and Vision*, London: Hodder and Stoughton, 1996.
11. As in Percy, Martyn, *Words, Wonders and Power: Understanding Contemporary Christian Fundamentalism and Revivalism*, London: SPCK, 1996.
12. As in Tidball, Derek, *Who Are the Evangelicals?* London: Marshall Pickering, 1994.

conditionalism, while disagreeing with the majority, have done so from within the community, and on behalf of the community, and will remain within the community even if it finally rejects their convictions on this specific point.

This four-fold assessment of the evangelical debate on hell crystallises what has been clear throughout this report: namely, that while the differences between traditionalists and conditionalists are significant and heartfelt, these two groups still have a great deal in common – not only in general terms but also specifically in relation to the fate of the unrighteous. In the final section of this report, we shall attempt to define these divergences and convergences with respect to the parameters of evangelicalism. We shall also make recommendations on how the doctrine of hell may be applied to contemporary church life and mission.

10

Conclusions and Recommendations

The following conclusions and recommendations rest on core evangelical convictions about God and his Word. These convictions may be summarised as follows:

- Matters relating to hell, as much as to creation, revelation and redemption, are subject to the sovereignty and grace of God the Father, God the Son and God the Holy Spirit.
- Christian teaching on hell must be derived above all from Scripture, since Scripture is entirely trustworthy and supremely authoritative in all matters of faith and conduct.
- In the contemporary interpretation of Scriptural teaching on hell, as on other doctrines, we look to the Holy Spirit to illuminate us and lead us into the truth.
- In reflecting on the doctrine of hell, we look for practical application to the church's urgent task of mission and evangelism.

1. All human beings must face death. In this, they are distinguished from God himself, and from the holy angels. Our mortality is a consequence of sin, which in turn derives from humanity's original rebellion against God (Ecc. 7:2; Rom. 5:12ff.).

2. After death, all human beings will be resurrected to face the final judgment of God (John 5:25–29; Heb.9:27; Rev. 20:13). Those who through grace have been justified by faith in Jesus Christ will be received into eternal glory, while those who have refused him will be condemned to hell (Phil. 3:20; 1 Pet. 1:4–9; John 12:48). Although justification is by faith through grace (Rom. 5:1, Gal. 3:24), the final judgment itself will take account of how faith has been lived out (Matt. 19:28f.; 25:31–46; 2 Cor. 5:10; Rev. 20:11–15).

3. God has revealed no other way to salvation and eternal life apart from through Jesus Christ (John 14:6; Acts 4:12).

4. In his sovereignty, God might save some who have not explicitly professed faith in Jesus Christ. The most likely groups from which such people might come are those who through no fault of their own have been unable to hear or respond to the gospel – e.g. the unevangelised, children who die in infancy, or those who have severe mental disabilities. While such people and others might receive the mercy of God in salvation, we are not at liberty to presume that any specific individual will be saved apart from professing faith in Jesus Christ. In particular, we can find no convincing warrant in Scripture for 'post-mortem' or 'second chance' repentance. We also reject the teaching of universalism, which holds that all will be saved regardless of their commitment to Christ (Rom. 2:12–16; Luke 1:15; 18:15–17; Rom. 10:9–13; Matt. 7:13).

5. Bearing 4 in mind, Christians should conduct mission and evangelism on the basis that proclamation and demonstration of the gospel are the definitive means by which God intends to save people and make disciples of all nations. Although the gospel is fundamentally 'good news' about the love of God revealed in Jesus Christ, it is appropriate that Christian witness should also include the message of divine judgment and hell (Matt. 28:18–20; Rom. 10:14–15; Acts 10:42; 17:31).

6. Hell is more than mere annihilation at the point of death. Rather, death will lead on to resurrection and final judgment to either heaven or hell (1 Cor. 15:1–58; John 5:25–9; Rev. 20:11–14).

7. As well as separation from God, hell involves severe punishment. Scripture depicts this punishment in various ways, using both psychological and physical terminology. Although this terminology is often metaphorical and although we should be wary of inferring more detail about hell than Scripture itself affords, hell is a *conscious* experience of rejection and torment (Matt. 8:12, 13:42, 24:51; Luke 13:28, 16:23).

8. There are degrees of punishment and suffering in hell related to the severity of sins committed on earth. We should, however, be wary of speculating on how exactly the correlation between sins committed and penalties imposed will operate (Luke 10:12, 12:47f.).

9. The Bible describes hell as a realm of destruction. Evangelicals, however, diverge on whether this destruction applies to the actual *existence* of individual sinners (eventual annihilation), or to the *quality of their relationship with God* (eternal conscious punishment). Although Scripture frequently presents God's ultimate punishment for sin as 'death', the meaning of 'death' in Scripture is not confined merely to the cessation of earthly life, and is often used to convey long-term spiritual estrangement from God (Matt. 7:13, 10:28; John 5:16; Eph. 2:1).

10. Evangelicals diverge on whether hell is eternal in *duration* or *effect* – that is, whether an individual's punishment in hell will literally go on 'for ever', as a ceaseless conscious experience, or whether it will end in a destruction which will be 'forever', in the sense of being final and irreversible. It should be acknowledged that both of these interpretations preserve the crucial principle that judgment is on the basis of sins committed in *this* life, and that when judgment is to hell,

it cannot be repealed (Matt. 25:41–6; Mark, 9:43–8; Luke 16:26).

11. God's purpose extends beyond judgment to the redemption of the cosmos. Evangelicals diverge on whether a place is preserved for hell in this new order of things, but it is important to stress that, either way, God's demands of justice will have been fully and perfectly met by this point (Rev. 20:14,21:4,cf.22:15).

12. We urge church leaders to present biblical teaching on hell to their congregations, and to relate it to their ongoing ministries of personal visitation, evangelism and social action.

13. We commend sensitivity and discernment in presenting the message of hell – particularly to those for whom commitment to Christ is uncertain or unrealised. Where such people are terminally ill, we urge a simple, compassionate presentation of the gospel, which may include mention of hell as appropriate and necessary. The same applies to relatives and friends of those approaching death.

14. When Christians have died, we encourage declaration of their heavenly inheritance in pastoral care of their bereaved relatives and friends, and in the conduct of their funerals or cremations.

15. Where the relationship of a deceased person to God has been unclear, or even apparently hostile, we would caution against explicit pronouncement on that person's eternal destiny. Rather, we urge those caring for their bereaved friends or relatives, and those conducting their funerals or cremations, to commend the gospel of Christ, spelling out the eternal consequences of unbelief in more general terms as appropriate and necessary.

16. We encourage theological colleges and related Christian organisations to train church leaders to a high standard of

biblical preaching, teaching and pastoral care in matters related to hell. We are concerned that this difficult subject is too often avoided today, and that our mission and witness may be compromised as a result.

17. We urge evangelicals involved in religious education in schools to ensure that modules on Christianity include presentations on death, judgment, heaven and hell.

18. We recognise that the interpretation of hell as eternal conscious punishment is the one most widely attested by the Church in its historic formulation of doctrine and in its understanding of Scripture. We also recognise that it represents the classic, mainstream evangelical position. We note that hell is defined explicitly as 'eternal punishment' by the doctrinal bases of the British Evangelical Council and the Evangelical Movement of Wales, both of whom have representatives on ACUTE.

19. We recognise that the interpretation of hell in terms of conditional immortality is a significant minority evangelical view. Furthermore, we believe that the traditionalist-conditionalist debate on hell should be regarded as a secondary rather than a primary issue for evangelical theology. Although hell is a profoundly serious matter, we view the holding of either one of these two views of it over against the other to be neither essential in respect of Christian doctrine, nor finally definitive of what it means to be an evangelical Christian.

20. We understand the current Evangelical Alliance Basis of Faith to allow both traditionalist and conditionalist interpretations of hell. The current form of the EA Basis, however, makes it difficult to draw definitive conclusions on this matter, because it has no specific clause devoted to general resurrection, final judgment and heaven and hell *as such*. We believe that the inclusion of such a clause might be helpful, not least as

a means of clarifying what we take to be an implicit openness to conditionalism in the present wording of the Basis.

21. We appreciate the concerns of some that the influence of conditionalist theology has grown within evangelicalism in recent years, but recognise that the majority of those who have published as 'evangelical conditionalists' have strong evangelical credentials, and have in particular demonstrated a genuine regard for the authority of Scripture.

22. We encourage traditionalist and conditionalist evangelicals to pursue agreement on the matter of hell, rather than merely acquiescing in their disagreement. As they do so, we call upon them to maintain constructive dialogue and respectful relationships, even when their differences seem intractable. To these ends, we commend our report for consideration, discussion and implementation.

Appendix: The Doctrine of Hell in Pan-Evangelical Confessions

The World's Evangelical Alliance (1846)

The Alliance was formed in London by delegates from Britain, mainland Europe and North America. Clause 8 of its founding Basis of Faith affirmed:

> The immortality of the Soul, the Resurrection of the Body, the Judgment of the World by our Lord Jesus Christ, with the Eternal Blessedness of the Righteous, and the Eternal Punishment of the wicked.

The Evangelical Alliance (1970)

The international Alliance which came together in 1846 soon devolved down into national bodies. The UK Alliance revised the 1846 Basis between 1967–70. The doctrine of hell was removed to these two affirmations, 3 and 4, where it became implicit rather than explicit:

> The universal sinfulness and guilt of fallen man, making him subject to God's wrath and condemnation.

> The substitutionary sacrifice of the incarnate Son of God, as the sole and all-sufficient ground of our redemption from the guilt and power of sin, and from its eternal consequences.

The World Evangelical Fellowship (1951)

Clause 7 of the WEF Statement affirms:

> The resurrection of both the saved and the lost; they that are saved unto the resurrection of life, and they that are lost unto the resurrection of damnation.

British Evangelical Council (1953)

Clause 6 of the Doctrinal Basis affirms:

> The resurrection of the body, the judgment of the world by our Lord Jesus Christ, the everlasting blessedness of the saved and the everlasting punishment of the lost.

The Evangelical Movement of Wales (1955)

Clause 3 of the Constitution states:

> As the righteous Judge [Christ] will divide all men into two, and only two, categories: the saved and the lost. Those whose faith is in Christ will be saved eternally, and will enter into the joy of their Lord, sharing with Him His inheritance in heaven. The unbelieving will be condemned by Him to hell, where eternally they will be punished for their sins under the righteous judgment of God.

The Fellowship of Independent Evangelical Churches (1922)

Clause 9 of the Doctrinal Basis reads:

> The Lord Jesus Christ will return in glory. He will raise the dead and judge the world in righteousness. The wicked he will send to eternal punishment and the righteous will be welcomed into a life of eternal joy in fellowship with God. God will make all things new and will be glorified for ever.

Universities and Colleges Christian Fellowship (1981)

From its formation in 1928 until 1981, UCCF worked with a doctrinal basis which made no explicit mention of hell. In 1981, the basis was revised and the following affirmation (k) was inserted:

> The future personal return of the Lord Jesus Christ, who will judge all men, executing God's just condemnation on the impenitent and receiving the redeemed to eternal glory.

A 'complementary' version of the basis was adopted in 1995. It expresses the same affirmation in the following words:

> The Lord Jesus will return in person, to judge everyone, to execute God's just condemnation on those who have not repented and to receive the redeemed to eternal glory.

Bibliography

Footnote abbreviations of more frequently cited works shown in bold type.

Aldwinckle, R., *Death in the Secular City: Life after Death in Contemporary Theology and Philosophy*, Grand Rapids: W.B. Eerdmans, 1974.

Aquinas, Thomas, *On the Truth of the Catholic Faith, Summa Contra Gentiles*, Trans. Vernon J. Bourke, Garden City, NJ: Doubleday, 1956.

Aquinas, Thomas, *Summa Theologiae*, Blackfriars. New York: McGraw-Hill, 1974. **Summa.**

Arnobius, *The Seven Books of Arnobius Adversus Gentes*, Ante-Nicene Christian Library, vol. 19; Edinburgh: T&T Clark, 1871.

Augustine, *Exposition on the Book of Psalms*, Peabody, Mass.: Hendrikson, 1995.

Augustine, *City of God*, Trans. Henry Bettenson. Harmondsworth: Penguin, 1984. **City of God**.

Barth, Karl, *Church Dogmatics*, Trans. G.W. Bromiley & T.F. Torrance. Edinburgh: T&T Clark, 1956–1977. **CD.**

Basil of Caesarea, *Regulae Brevius Tractatae ('The Shorter Rules')* in W.K.L. Clarke (ed., trans.) *The Ascetic Works of St. Basil*, London: SPCK, 1925, pp. 229–352.

Bauckham, R., 'Universalism: A Historical Survey', *Themelios* 4:2 (January 1979).

Bauckham, R., *Jude, 2 Peter*, Waco: Word, 1983.

Bauckham, R., 'Early Jewish Visions of Hell', *Journal of Theological Studies*, 41.2, (1990), 357–85.

Bauckham, R., 'The Rich Man and Lazarus: The Parable and the Parallels', *NTS* 37, 1991, 226–27.

Bauckham, R., 'Descent to the Underworld', *ABD* (1992) 2:145–59.

Bauckham, R., 'Visiting Places of the Dead in the Extra-Canonical Apocalypses', *Proceedings of the Irish Biblical Association*, 18, 1995, 84.

Bauckham, R., 'Life, Death and the Afterlife in Second Temple Judaism', in R.L. Longenecker (ed.), *Life in the Face of Death: The Resurrection Message of the New Testament*, Grand Rapids: Eerdmans, 1998, pp. 80–95.

Beasley-Murray, George R., *John*, Waco: Word, 1987.

Bebbington, D.W., *Evangelicalism in Modern Britain: A History from the 1730s to the 1980s*, London: Unwin Hyman, 1989. **Evangelicalism**.

Berkhof, Louis, *Reformed Dogmatics. Vol 2*, Grand Rapids: Eerdmans, 1932.

Berkouwer, G.C., *The Triumph of Grace in the Theology of Karl Barth*, Grand Rapids: Eerdmans, 1956.

Berkouwer, G.C., *Return of Christ*, Grand Rapids: Eerdmans, 1972.

Bettenson, Henry (ed., trans.), *The Early Christian Fathers*, Oxford/New York: Oxford University Press, 1956. **Early Christian Fathers.**

Bettenson, Henry (ed., trans.), *The Later Christian Fathers*, Oxford/New York: Oxford University Press, 1970. **Later Christian Fathers.**

Bloesch, D.G., *Essentials of Evangelical Theology, Vol 2*, San Francisco: Harper Row, 1979.

Bloesch, D.G., 'Descent into Hell (Hades)' in Walter A. Elwell (ed.), *Evangelical Dictionary of Theology*, Exeter: Paternoster, 1984, pp. 313–5.

Blanchard, John, *Whatever Happened to Hell?* Darlington: Evangelical Press, 1993. **Whatever.**

Blomberg, Craig, 'Eschatology and the Church: Some New Testament Perspectives', *Themelios* 23:3 (1998), 3–26.

Blum, Edwin, 'Shall You Not Surely Die?' *Themelios* 4:2 (1979), 58–61.

Boettner, Lorraine, *The Reformed Doctrine of Predestination*, Phillipsburg: NJ.: Presbyterian and Reformed Publishing Co., 1992.

Bonda, Jan, *The One Purpose of God: An Answer to the Doctrine of Eternal Punishment*, Grand Rapids: Eerdmans, 1998 [1993]. **One Purpose.**

Bray, Gerald, 'Hell: Eternal Punishment or Total Annihilation?' *Evangel* 10:2 (Summer 1992), 19–24.

Bromiley, Geoffrey W., *Introduction to the Theology of Karl Barth*, Edinburgh: T&T Clark, 1979.

Brown, Harold, 'Will the Lost Suffer Forever?' *Criswell Theological Review*, 4.2 (1990).

Buchanan, Alex, *Heaven and Hell*, Tonbridge: Sovereign World, 1995.

Burns, Norman T., *Christian Mortalism from Tyndale to Milton*, Cambridge, Mass.: Harvard University Press, 1972.

Caesarius, Saint (Archbishop of Arles), *Sermons (3 Vols)*, Trans. Mary

Magdeleine Muller. Washington DC: Catholic University of America Press, 1956–1973.

Calver, Clive and Warner, Rob, *Together We Stand: Evangelical Convictions, Unity and Vision*, London: Hodder & Stoughton, 1996.

Calvin, John, *Institutes of Christian Religion*, Trans. F.L. Battles, Philadelphia: The Westminster Press, 1960. **Institutes.**

Cameron, Euan, *The European Reformation*, Oxford: Oxford University Press, 1991.

Carson, D.A., *How Long O Lord?: Reflections On Suffering And Evil*, Leicester: IVP, 1990.

Carson, D.A., *The Gagging of God: Christianity Confronts Pluralism*, Leicester: Apollos, 1996. **Gagging of God.**

Catherine of Genoa, 'Treatise on Purgatory', in, Unile Bonzi da Genova (ed.) *Edizione Critica dei Manoscritti Cateriniani*, Genoa: Marietti, n.d.

Clarke, Eric & Sanderson, Ruth, *Aid to Watchtower Understanding*, Faversham: Christian Information Outreach, n.d.

Clement of Alexandria, *Stromateis*, Trans. P. Wood. Washington DC: Catholic University of America Press, 1991.

Colwell, John, 'The Contemporaneity of Divine Decision: Reflections on Barth's Denial of "Universalism", in Cameron, Nigel de S. (ed.), *Universalism and the Doctrine of Hell'*, Carlisle: Paternoster, 1992, pp. 139–160. **Divine Decision.**

Constable, H., *Hades; or the Intermediate State of Man (2nd. Edn.)*, London: Kellaway and Co., 1875.

Cooper, J.W., *Body, Soul and the Life Everlasting*, Grand Rapids: Eerdmans, 1989.

Cotterell, Peter, *Mission and Meaninglessness*, London: SPCK, 1990.

Cotterell, Peter, *Dealing with Death: A Christian Perspective*, London: Scripture Union, 1994.

Creed, H.M., *St. Luke*, London: Macmillan, 1930.

Crockett, William (ed.), *Four Views on Hell*, Grand Rapids: Zondervan, 1992. **Four Views.**

Cyril of Jerusalem, *Catechetical Lectures (Catechesis) (2 Vols)*, Trans. Leo P. McCauley & Anthony A. Stephenson. Washington DC: Catholic University of America Press, 1969–1970.

Daley, Brian E., *The Hope of the Early Church: A Handbook of Patristic Eschatology*, Cambridge: Cambridge University Press, 1991. **Hope.**

Davies, Eryl, *Truth Under Attack: Cults and Contemporary Religions (2nd. Edn.)*, Darlington: Evangelical Press, 1995. **Truth Under Attack.**

Dillenberger, John, (ed.) *Martin Luther: Selections from His Writings*, New York: Anchor, 1961.

DiNiola, J., *The Diversity of Religions: A Christian Perspective*, Washington DC: The Catholic University Press, 1992.

Dixon, Larry, *The Other Side of the Good News: Confronting Contemporary Challenges to Jesus' Teaching on Hell*, Wheaton, Ill.: Bridgepoint, 1992. **Other Side.**

Dowsett, Dick, *God, That's Not Fair!* Carlisle: OM Publishing, 1998 [1982]. **Not Fair.**

Dunn, J.D.G., *Word Biblical Commentary: Romans 1–8*, Dallas: Word, 1988.

Du Toit, D.A., 'Descensus and Universalism: Some Historical Patterns of Interpretation', in Cameron, Nigel M. de S. (ed.), *Universalism and the Doctrine of Hell*, Carlisle: Paternoster, 1992, pp. 73–92.

Edwards, Jonathan, *On Knowing Christ*, Edinburgh: Banner of Truth Trust, 1990.

Eller, David B., 'Universalism', in Walter A. Elwell (ed.), *Evangelical Dictionary of Theology*, Exeter: Paternoster, 1984. **Universalism.**

Ellis, Earle, 'New Testament Teaching on Hell', in K.E. Brower & M.W. Elliott (eds.), *'The Reader Must Understand': Eschatology in Bible and Theology*, Leicester: Apollos, 1997, pp. 199–219. **New Testament Teaching.**

Evans, Stephen T., *Risen Indeed: A Christian Philosophy of Resurrection*, Grand Rapids: Eerdmans, 1993.

Fernando, Ajith, *Crucial Questions About Hell*, Eastbourne: Kingsway, 1991. **Crucial Questions.**

Ferré Nels F.S., *The Christian Understanding of God*, London: SCM Press, 1951.

Fletcher, Caroline, 'Hell in the New Testament and Church History', Unpublished M.Phil, University of Sheffield, 1997. **Hell.**

Frame, J.M., 'Second Chance', in Walter A. Elwell, *Evangelical Dictionary of Theology*, Exeter: Paternoster, 1984, p. 991. **Second Chance.**

France, R.T., 'Exegesis in Practice: Two Examples', in I. Howard Marshall (ed.), *New Testament Interpretation*, Exeter: Paternoster, 1977, pp. 252–81.

Froom, L.E., *The Conditionalist Faith of our Fathers*, Washington: Herald and Review Publishing Association, 1965, 1966 (2 Vols.). **Conditionalist Faith.**

Fudge, Edward William, *The Fire That Consumes: The Biblical Case for Conditional Immortality (Revised Edn.)*, Carlisle: Paternoster, 1994 [1982]. **Fire.**

General Medical Council, *Good Medical Practice* (2nd Edn.), London, 1998.

Gerstner, John, *Repent or Perish*, Ligonier, PA.: Soli Deo Gloria, 1990. **Repent or Perish.**

Gray, Tony, 'Destroyed For Ever: An Examination of the Debates Concerning Annihilation and Conditional Immortality', *Themelios* 21:2 (January 1996), 14–18. **Destroyed Forever.**

Green, Michael, *Evangelism Through the Local Church*, London: Hodder & Stoughton, 1990.

Gregory the Great, *Dialogia*, in *Sources Chretiennes, Vol. 265*, Ed. Albert de Vogue. Paris: Cerf, 1980.

Gregory of Nyssa, 'Select Writings and Letters', in *Nicene and Post-Nicene Fathers V,* Oxford: Oxford University Press, 1893.

Grudem, Wayne, *Systematic Theology*, Leicester, IVP, 1994.

Guillebaud, H.E., *The Righteous Judge: A Study of the Biblical Doctrine of Everlasting Punishment*, Taunton: Phoenix,1964. **Righteous Judge.**

Haring, Hermann & Metz, Johann-Baptist (eds.), *Reincarnation or Resurrection?* Concilium, 1993 (5).

Harmon, Kendall, 'The Case Against Conditionalism', in Cameron, Nigel M. de S. (ed.), *Universalism and the Doctrine of Hell*, Carlisle: Paternoster, 1992, pp. 193–224. **Case Against Conditionalism.**

Harris, M.J., *Raised Immortal*, London: Marshall, Morgan and Scott, 1983.

Harris, R.L., 'Why Hebrew *She'ol* was translated "grave"', in K.L. Barker (ed.), *The Making of a Contemporary Translation*, London: Hodder & Stoughton, 1987, pp. 75–92.

Harris, R.L., 'The Meaning of the Word Sheol as Shown by Parallels in Poetic Texts', *Bulletin of the Evangelical Theological Society* 4 (1961), 129–35.

Harris, R.L., 'she'ol', in R.L. Harris, G.L. Archer & B.K. Waltke (eds.), *Theological Wordbook of the Old Testament*, Chicago: Moody Press, 1980.

Hart, Trevor, 'Universalism: Two Distinct Types', in Cameron, Nigel M. de S. (ed.), *Universalism and the Doctrine of Hell*, Carlisle: Paternoster, 1992, pp. 1–34. **Universalism.**

Hayes, Zachary, 'The Purgatorial View', in William Crockett (ed.), *Four Views on Hell*, Grand Rapids: Zondervan, 1992, pp. 91–118. **Purgatorial View.**

Head, Peter M., 'The Duration of Divine Judgment in the New Testament', in K.E. Brower & M.W. Elliott (eds.), *'The Reader Must Understand': Eschatology in Bible and Theology*, Leicester: IVP, 1997, pp. 221–227. **Duration.**

Helm, Paul, *The Last Things: Death, Judgment, Heaven and Hell*, Edinburgh: Banner of Truth, 1989. **Last Things.**

Hick, John, *Death and Eternal Life*, London: Collins, 1976. (Reprinted Basingstoke: Macmillan, 1985). **Death and Eternal Life.**

Hick, John, *Evil and the God of Love (2nd. Edn.)*, London, Macmillan, 1977 [1966].

Hick, John, 'The Non-Absoluteness of Christianity', in J. Hick and P. Knitter (eds), *The Myth of Christian Uniqueness. Toward a Pluralistic Theology of Religions*, New York: Orbis, 1987.

Hinton, John, *Dying*, Harmondsworth: Pelican, 1967.

Hoekema, Anthony A., *The Bible and the Future*, Exeter: Paternoster, 1979. **Future.**

Howe, Q. Jnr., *Reincarnation for the Christian*, Philadelphia: Theosophical Publishing House, 1994.

Hughes, P.E., *The True Image: The Origin and Destiny of Man in Christ*, Leicester: IVP, 1989. **True Image.**

Hunter, James Davison, *Evangelicalism: The Coming Generation*, Chicago/London: University of Chicago Press, 1987.

Jathanna, Origen, *The Decisiveness of the Christ-Event and the Universality of Christianity in a World of Religious Plurality*, Berne: Peter Lang, 1982.

Jerome, *In Isaiam (Commentary on Isaiah). Corpus Christianum Series Latina*, 73.

John Chrysostom, *Homilies on the First Epistle of St. Paul to the Corinthians*, Oxford: Oxford University Press, Library of the Fathers, 1839.

Johnston, P.S., ' "Left in Hell"? Psalm 16, Sheol and the Holy One', in P.E. Satterthwaite *et al.* (ed.), *The Lord's Anointed: Interpretation of Old Testament Messianic Texts*, Carlisle: Paternoster, pp. 213–222.

Jukes, Andrew, *The Second Death and the Restitution of All Things*, Hornchurch: Scripture Studies Concern/Concordant, 1976 [Originally Published, 1867].

Justin Martyr, 'First & Second Apology', ed. & trans. Thomas B. Falls in *Saint Justin Martyr*, Washington DC: Catholic University of America Press, 1948, pp. 23–138.

Justin Martyr, 'Dialogue with Trypho', ed. & trans. Thomas B. Falls in *Saint Justin Martyr*, Washington DC: Catholic University of America Press, 1948, pp. 139–368.

Kendall, R.T., *Once Saved, Always Saved*, Belfast: Ambassador, [1983] 1992.

Kessler, J.B.A. Jnr., *A Study of the Evangelical Alliance in Great Britain*, Goes: Oosterbaan & Le Cointre, 1968. **Evangelical Alliance.**

Knight, H.K. III, *A Future for Truth: Evangelical Theology in a Postmodern World*, Nashville: Abingdon Press, 1997.

Kübler-Ross, Elisabeth, *On Death and Dying*, New York: Macmillan, 1969.

Lactantius, *The Divine Institutes, Books I-IV,* ed. & trans. Mary Francis MacDonald. Washington DC: Catholic University of America Press, 1964.

Le Goff, J. *The Birth of Purgatory,* Trans. A. Goldhammer. Chicago: University of Chicago Press, 1984. **Purgatory.**

Leith, John. H. (ed.), *Creeds of the Churches (Third Edition),* Louisville: John Knox Press, 1982.

Lewis, C.S., *The Problem of Pain,* Glasgow: Fount, 1977 [1940]. **Problem of Pain.**

Lewis, C.S., *The Great Divorce,* Glasgow: Fontana, 1972 [1946]. **Great Divorce.**

Lightfoot, J.B., Holmes, M.W. & Harmer, J.R., *The Apostolic Fathers,* Grand Rapids: Baker Book House, 1998 (Originally London, 1885).

Luther, Martin, 'Lectures on Titus, Philemon and Hebrews', *Luther's Works,* 29. Ed. Jaroslav Pelikan & Walter A. Hansen, Missouri: Concordia, 1968, pp. 176-7.

Luther, Martin, *Luther's Works: Career of the Reformer I,* Ed. H.J. Grimm, *Luther's Works,* 31. Philadelphia: Fortress Press, 1957.

McGrath, Alister E., *Roots that Refresh: A Celebration of Reformation Spirituality,* London: Hodder & Stoughton, 1992.

McGrath, Alister E., *Evangelicalism and the Future of Christianity,* London: Hodder & Stoughton, 1994.

McGrath, Alister E., *A Passion for Truth: The Intellectual Coherence of Evangelicalism,* Leicester: Apollos, 1996.

MacGregor, Geddes., *Reincarnation as a Christian Hope,* London: Macmillan, 1982.

Macquarrie, John, *Christian Hope,* Oxford: Mowbray, 1978.

Maurice, F.D., *Theological Essays (2nd. Edn.),* London: James Clarke & Co, Ltd., 1853.

Marsden, George M., *Reforming Fundamentalism: Fuller Seminary and the New Evangelicalism,* Grand Rapids: Eerdmans, 1987.

Marshall, I. Howard, *The Gospel of Luke,* Exeter: Paternoster, 1978. **Luke.**

Milne, Bruce, A., *Know the Truth,* Leicester: IVP, 1982.

Moltmann, Jürgen, 'The Logic of Hell' in Bauckham, Richard (ed.), *God Will Be All in All: The Eschatology of Jürgen Moltmann,* Edinburgh: T&T Clark, 1999.

Morey, R.A., *Death and the Afterlife,* Minneapolis: Bethany, 1984.

Motyer, Alec, *After Death (Revised Edn.),* Fearn: Christian Focus, 1996. **After Death.**

Noll, Mark A. (ed.), *Confessions and Catechisms of the Reformation*, Leicester: Apollos, 1991.

Noll, Mark A. *The Scandal of the Evangelical Mind*, Leicester: IVP, 1994.

Nash, Ronald H. *When A Baby Dies: Answers to Comfort Grieving Parents*, Grand Rapids: Zondervan, 1999. **When a Baby Dies.**

North, Brownlow, *The Rich Man and Lazarus: An Exposition of Luke 16:19–31*, Edinburgh: The Banner of Truth Trust, 1979 [1859].

Origen, *De Principiis (On First Principles)*, Trans. G.W. Butterworth. London: SPCK, 1936. **De Principiis.**

Packer, J.I. *The Problem of Eternal Punishment*, Disley: Orthos, 1990. **Eternal Punishment.**

Paternoster, M., *Thou Art There Also*, London: SPCK, 1967.

Pawson, David, *The Road to Hell*, London: Hodder & Stoughton, 1992. **Road to Hell.**

Pawson, David, *Once Saved, Always Saved?* London: Hodder & Stoughton, 1996.

Percy, Martyn, *Words, Wonders and Power: Understanding Contemporary Christian Fundamentalism and Revivalism*, London: SPCK, 1996.

Peterson, R.A., *Hell on Trial: The Case for Eternal Punishment*, Phillipsburg: P&R Publishing, 1995. **Hell on Trial.**

Pinnock, Clark H. 'Fire then Nothing', *Christianity Today*, 20th March 1987.

Pinnock, Clark H., 'The Finality of Christ in a World of Religions', in Mark A. Noll & David F. Wells (eds.), *Christian Faith and Practice in the Modern World*, Grand Rapids: Eerdmans, 1988, pp. 152–170. **Finality.**

Pinnock, Clark H. & Brow, Robert C., *Unbounded Love: A Good News Theology for the 21st Century*, Carlisle: Paternoster, 1994. **Unbounded Love.**

Powys, David, 'The Nineteenth and Twentieth Century Debates about Hell and Universalism', in Nigel M. De S. Cameron (ed.), *Universalism and the Doctrine of Hell*, Carlisle: Paternoster 1992, pp. 93–138. **Hell and Universalism.**

Powys, David, *'Hell': A Hard Look at a Hard Question*, Carlisle: Paternoster, 1997. **Hard Look.**

Punt, Neal, *Unconditional Good News: Toward an Understanding of Biblical Universalism*, Grand Rapids: Eerdmans, 1980. **Good News.**

Roberts, Alexander & Donaldson, James (ed.), *The Ante-Nicene Fathers*, Grand Rapids: Eerdmans, 1973. **Ante-Nicene Fathers.**

Robinson, John A.T., *In the End, God*, London: Collins, 1968. **In the End.**

Rowell, Geoffrey, *Hell and The Victorians*, Oxford: Clarendon, 1974. **Hell and the Victorians.**

Sanders, E.P., *Paul And Palestinian Judaism*, London: SCM, 1997.

Shedd, W.G.T., *Doctrine of Endless Punishment*, New York: Scribner, 1886. **Endless Punishment.**

Smith, Anthony M., *Gateway to Life: Death and Bereavement – Help and Hope Along the Journey*, Leicester: IVP, 1994.

Spanner, Douglas, 'Is Hell Forever?' *Churchman* 110:2, 1996, 107–120.

Stott, John & Edwards, David L., *Essentials: A Liberal-Evangelical Dialogue*, London: Hodder & Stoughton, 1988. **Essentials.**

Swinburne, R., *The Evolution of the Soul*, Oxford: Clarendon Press, 1986.

Talbott, Thomas, 'The New Testament and Universal Reconciliation'. *Christian Scholar's Review*, XXI: 4 (1992).

Tatian, *Address to the Greeks (Oratio ad Graecos)*, Trans. Molly Whittaker. Oxford: Clarendon Press, 1982.

Theophilus of Antioch, *Ad Autolycum*, ed. & trans. R.M. Grant. Oxford: Oxford University Press, 1970.

Thompson, Mark, *Saving the Heart: What is an Evangelical?* London: St Matthias Press, 1995.

Tidball, Derek J., *Who Are the Evangelicals?* London: Marshall Pickering, 1994.

Tillich, Paul, *Systematic Theology*, Welwyn, Herts.: James Nisbet & Co., 1968.

Toon, Peter, *Longing for the Heavenly Realm: The Missing Element in Modern Western Spirituality*, London: Hodder & Stoughton, 1986

Travis, Stephen H., *Christian Hope and the Future of Man*, Leicester: IVP, 1980. **Christian Hope.**

Travis, Stephen H., *I Believe in the Second Coming of Jesus*, London: Hodder & Stoughton, 1982. **Second Coming.**

Travis, Stephen H., *Christ and the Judgment of God: Divine Retribution in the New Testament*, Basingstoke: Marshall, Morgan and Scott, 1986. **Christ and the Judgment of God.**

Troeltsch, Ernst, *The Absoluteness of Christianity and the History of Religion*, London: SCM Press, 1972. [Originally published as *The Absolute Validity of Christianity*, London, 1901].

Tucker, Ruth: *Strange Gospels*, London: Marshall Pickering, 1989.

Walker, D.P., *The Decline of Hell: Seventeenth Century Discussions of Eternal Torment*, London: Routledge & Kegan Paul, 1964.

Walvoord, John F., 'Response to Zachary J. Hayes' in William Crockett (ed.), *Four Views on Hell*, Grand Rapids: Zondervan, 1992, pp. 119–121. **Response.**

Weatherhead, Leslie D., *The Christian Agnostic*, London: Hodder & Stoughton, 1965.

Weatherhead, Leslie D., *Life Begins at Death*, Nutfield: Denham House Press, 1969.

Wells, David, *No Place for Truth, or Whatever Happened to Evangelical Theology?* Leicester: IVP, 1993.

Wenham, John W., *The Goodness of God*, Leicester: IVP, 1974. Later reprinted as *The Enigma of Evil*, 1985. **Goodness.**

Wenham, John W., 'The Case for Conditional Immortality', in Cameron, Nigel M. de S. (ed.), *Universalism and the Doctrine of Hell*, Carlisle: Paternoster, 1992, pp. 161–91. **Conditional Immortality.**

Wenham, John W., *Facing Hell: An Autobiography 1913–1996*, Carlisle: Paternoster, 1998. **Facing Hell.**

Wescott, Brooke Fosse, *The Gospel According to St. John*, Grand Rapids: Baker Book House, 1908 [1980].

White, Vernon, *Atonement and Incarnation*, Cambridge: Cambridge University Press, 1991.

Wilbur, E.M., *A History of Unitarianism: Socinianism and Its Antecedents*, Cambridge: Cambridge University Press, 1952.

Wink, Walter, *Unmasking the Powers*, Philadelphia: Fortress Press, 1986.

Wolfson, H.A., 'Notes on Patristic Philosophy', *Harvard Theological Review* 57, no. 2 (April 1964), 119–132.

Wolfson, H.A., 'Immortality and Resurrection in the Philosophy of the Church Fathers', in Krister Stendahl (ed.), *Immortality and Resurrection*, New York: Macmillan, 1965.

Wright, N.T., 'Towards a Biblical View Of Universalism', *Themelios* 4:2, 1979, 54–58. **Universalism.**

Wright, Nigel, *The Radical Evangelical: Seeking a Place to Stand*, London: SPCK, 1996. **Radical Evangelical.**